SUN SIGNS

PAST LIVES

About the Author

Bernie Ashman has written for *Dell Horoscope, Astro Signs, Mountain Astrologer,* and *Welcome to Planet Earth* magazines. He has appeared on a number of television and radio shows, and lectures throughout the United States. He has also written the text for many astrological software programs. His other book include *Astrological Games People Play, RoadMap to Your Future,* and *SignMates.*

Bernie Ashman

Your Soul's Evolutionary Path

Llewellyn Publications
Woodbury, Minnesota

Book design by Steffani Sawyer
Book edited by Nicole Edman
Cover art © 2010 iStockphoto.com/Nic Taylor and Wrangel
Cover design by Ellen Lawson

Llewellyn is a registered trademark of Llewellyn Worldwide Ltd.

ISBN 978-0-7387-2107-1

Llewellyn Worldwide Ltd. does not participate in, endorse, or have any authority or responsibility concerning private business transactions between our authors and the public.

All mail addressed to the author is forwarded but the publisher cannot, unless specifically instructed by the author, give out an address or phone number.

Any Internet references contained in this work are current at publication time, but the publisher cannot guarantee that a specific location will continue to be maintained. Please refer to the publisher's website for links to authors' websites and other sources.

Llewellyn Publications
A Division of Llewellyn Worldwide Ltd.
2143 Wooddale Drive
Woodbury, MN 55125-2989

Printed in the United States of America

Other Books by Bernie Ashman

Astrological Games People Play
(ACS Publications, 1987)

RoadMap to Your Future: A Quick Guide to Progressions & Transits
(ACS Publications, 1994)

SignMates: Understanding the Games People Play
(Llewellyn, 2000)

Contents

Introduction

Welcome to a book that encourages you to be your own past-life detective. The wealth of information on the following pages will guide you into your inner landscape. This book is meant to awaken your creative passion to take advantage of opportunities in your outer world in this lifetime. The greater our inner understanding, the more we can experience and express our potential.

Past Lives

We live in a spiritual universe. Earth represents a stage upon which we can act out our potential. There is a key theory or philosophy at work in this book, which is that we have lived previous incarnations on planet Earth. Within us are memories from previous lives.

Our conscious mind does not recall our previous lives, but these memories are stored within us. If our mind isn't doing the remembering, then what is? Call it the soul, higher consciousness, tapping into the Collective Unconscious, or whatever concept suits you. The theory behind reincarnation is that the soul returns to Earth by taking on a new physical body. We get another chance to fulfill our potential. When we die, it's the soul that leaves the body behind and journeys forward, waiting for a chance to incarnate once again.

Karma and Freedom of Choice

There is a saying that "you reap what you sow." This is often referred to as the law of karma, or the great principle of cause and effect. There are actions and thoughts that defined us in other lives. They have guided us to where we are in the present. Some of these actions and thoughts (or tendencies) were positive influences, while others caused us to veer off-course in terms of growth. These past impressions don't really exert any control over us, though at times their pull can feel immense. The fundamental message of this book is that we have freedom of choice to create new options in our current life.

Evolutionary Path and Past-Life Patterns

Why do we reincarnate? The theory is that we are evolving. If we choose to learn from the past, each lifetime leads us farther along the evolutionary trail. Past-life patterns, or certain repetitive behaviors from previous incarnations, may have taken us down the wrong path. Our creative power is unleashed by confronting worn-out behaviors that no longer serve any useful purpose and by rising above their influences. There is a purpose each of us is trying to fulfill in life. It isn't so much that we are trying to erase our karma or past-life lessons, but the idea is to gain the wisdom and consciousness to make choices that advance our growth.

In a sense, each of us is trying to get attuned to our soul! We are attempting to rise to the level at which the soul operates. This takes self-understanding and reflection, which always comes back to finding emotional and mental balance. The information you will encounter in this book is intended to clarify a key reason for your incarnation. No one person or book has all of the answers, but every once in a while we come across more clues. Think of this book as helping to point you toward deeper reasons for your current incarnation.

It does not matter how many lifetimes we may have repeated a self-destructive or nonproductive pattern of behavior. *We can alter the influence of a pattern—even if it has been repeated over several lifetimes—*

and heal ourselves in this incarnation if we develop the necessary insight to find our way to brighter life paths.

There are no perfect people, so do not feel bad if you read something in the section for your birthday that seems negative. If we were all completely perfect with no lessons to learn, there would be no reason to incarnate. Don't you agree? Think of overcoming past-life patterns as homework. When you identify a thought pattern that has been holding you back, you are on the way to growth that can transform you. It feels liberating to let go of that negative energy!

What Is a Sun Sign?

Each of the twelve signs of the zodiac is created by the Sun's apparent path around Earth along what is known as the ecliptic. In the course of the Sun's apparent motion along the ecliptic, the Sun passes through the twelve zodiacal constellations, spending approximately thirty days in each constellation's space in the sky. One such revolution through the signs equals a year.

In astrology, the Sun symbolizes our ego. It denotes our willpower and the drive to express ourselves. It's the heart and center of our soul's way of being creative while we are here on Earth. Think of the signs as the psychological and spiritual clothing we adopt in order to pursue our goals and dreams. Our astrological sign is the vehicle through which our consciousness travels to realize our highest potential. *It's important to realize that your Sun sign symbolism is your response to some of your past-life patterns.* Your sign may not encompass all of the past patterns, but it does represent many vital ones to understand. Your Sun sign is more than symbolic of your current life creative self-expression; it contains much of the DNA holding your past-life pattern memory!

The Four Elements

Each of the twelve astrological signs belongs to an element: Fire, Air, Earth, and Water. The great psychologist Carl Jung wrote about four functions that correspond to the elements: *Emotion, Intellect, Sensation* (in terms of the physical senses), and *Intuition.* There are three signs belonging to each element.

Emotion is essentially the zeal of the *Fire-sign trilogy*: Aries, Leo, and Sagittarius. To act on impulse is typical of a Fire sign. Processing is not the top priority. A bit of the daredevil spirit and a love of adventure often encompass this elemental tendency. Learning patience is part of the path to wisdom.

Intellect belongs very much in the domain of the communication-focused and perception-oriented *Air-sign trilogy*: Gemini, Libra, and Aquarius. To think first and then act is true of Air. Mental ingenuity is at the fingertips of these three breezy signs. Gaining focus makes life's journey that much more flowing and enjoyable.

Sensations, such as taste and touch, match the experiential needs of the *Earth-sign trilogy*: Taurus, Virgo, and Capricorn. This pragmatic bunch has a "show me" type of demeanor. A desire to know the bottom line before taking chances is true of Earth signs. Discipline and follow-through often come standard with these three. This element is tuned into survival instincts. Adopting flexibility is the path to happiness.

Intuition definitely is associated with the feeling nature of the *Water-sign trilogy*: Cancer, Scorpio, and Pisces. These three often see what other signs don't, in terms of life's mysteries. Emotions run deep in this element. Balancing a strong imaging power with a clear sense of reality yields greater fulfillment.

Each of us is a mixture of the four elements, which becomes quite vivid if you get an astrological reading done professionally. Even without a full chart reading, you probably can sense which of the elements are more dominant in your self-expression.

Three Magical Zone Divisions of a Sign

This is going to be a technical explanation of how the signs are shown in the following chapters. If you don't like technical information, feel free to skip this section! As a writer, I am of course hoping you will take the time to read this brief discussion. The explanation will advance your understanding of the material in the sign chapters.

A sign can be divided into thirds or three sections known in astrology as *decanates*. In this book, the sections are referred to as *zones*. This means there are three zones to each sign. There are thirty days in each sign, which means there are ten days in each zone. Each zone is linked or associated with a secondary sign, *the sign zone ruler*, which might be different than your Sun sign! If you were born during the First Zone, or first ten days, of your sign, you will have the same secondary sign associated with your zone. In other words, if you are an Aries and were born on March 24, you will notice that the secondary ruler of your zone is also Aries. If you were born during the first ten days of a sign, you will have a strong repeating theme in your sign influence. You are a "double" in this sign.

The ruler of a sign zone is always in the same element as the Sun sign. As stated in the element discussion, there are three signs belonging to each element. So for example, if your Sun sign is fiery Aries, your secondary sign will either be Aries, Leo, or Sagittarius, from the Fire-sign trio. If your Sun sign is airy Gemini, your secondary sign will either be Gemini, Libra, or Aquarius, from the Air-sign trio. If your Sun sign is earthy Taurus, your secondary sign will either be Taurus, Virgo, or Capricorn, from the Earth-sign trio. If your Sun sign is watery Cancer, your secondary sign will either be Cancer, Scorpio, or Pisces, from the Water-sign trio.

The past-life patterns are described in each chapter according to each sign's zones. It's easy to locate your own sign discussion because you only need to locate the zone containing your birthday. For instance, someone born on March 24 would look in the Aries chapter and find their own section between the days of March 21 and March 30, or the First Zone of Aries.

Birth Date	Sign	Zone	Zone Ruler	Element, Energy
3/21–3/30	Aries	First	Aries	Fire, Cardinal
3/31–4/9	Aries	Second	Leo	Fire, Fixed
4/10–4/19	Aries	Third	Sagittarius	Fire, Mutable
4/20–4/29	Taurus	First	Taurus	Earth, Fixed
4/30–5/9	Taurus	Second	Virgo	Earth, Mutable
5/10–5/20	Taurus	Third	Capricorn	Earth, Cardinal
5/21–5/30	Gemini	First	Gemini	Air, Mutable
5/31–6/10	Gemini	Second	Libra	Air, Cardinal
6/11–6/21	Gemini	Third	Aquarius	Air, Fixed
6/22–7/1	Cancer	First	Cancer	Water, Cardinal
7/2–7/11	Cancer	Second	Scorpio	Water, Fixed
7/12–7/21	Cancer	Third	Pisces	Water, Mutable
7/22–7/31	Leo	First	Leo	Fire, Fixed
8/1–8/10	Leo	Second	Sagittarius	Fire, Mutable
8/11–8/21	Leo	Third	Aries	Fire, Cardinal
8/22–8/31	Virgo	First	Virgo	Earth, Mutable
9/1–9/10	Virgo	Second	Capricorn	Earth, Cardinal
9/11–9/21	Virgo	Third	Taurus	Earth, Fixed
9/22–10/1	Libra	First	Libra	Air, Cardinal
10/2–10/11	Libra	Second	Aquarius	Air, Fixed
10/12–10/21	Libra	Third	Gemini	Air, Mutable
10/22–10/31	Scorpio	First	Scorpio	Water, Fixed
11/1–11/10	Scorpio	Second	Pisces	Water, Mutable
11/11–11/20	Scorpio	Third	Cancer	Water, Cardinal
11/21–11/30	Sagittarius	First	Sagittarius	Fire, Mutable
12/1–12/10	Sagittarius	Second	Aries	Fire, Cardinal
12/11–12/20	Sagittarius	Third	Leo	Fire, Fixed
12/21–12/30	Capricorn	First	Capricorn	Earth, Cardinal
12/31–1/9	Capricorn	Second	Taurus	Earth, Fixed
1/10–1/19	Capricorn	Third	Virgo	Earth, Mutable
1/20–1/29	Aquarius	First	Aquarius	Air, Fixed
1/30–2/8	Aquarius	Second	Gemini	Air, Mutable
2/9–2/18	Aquarius	Third	Libra	Air, Cardinal
2/19–2/28	Pisces	First	Pisces	Water, Mutable
2/29–3/10	Pisces	Second	Cancer	Water, Cardinal
3/11–3/20	Pisces	Third	Scorpio	Water, Fixed

The Zone Energy Fields

So remember, your particular zone is ruled by a secondary sign of the same element. The secondary sign can further be classified according to what I call an *energy field*. There are Cardinal, Fixed, and Mutable signs. The astrological year, unlike the calendar year, begins on March 21 with Aries and runs through to Pisces. The Cardinal signs are the first signs of their element: Aries, Cancer, Libra, and Capricorn. The Fixed signs are the second signs of their element: Taurus, Leo, Scorpio, and Aquarius. The Mutable signs are the last signs of their element: Gemini, Virgo, Sagittarius, and Pisces. You will notice that each sign has three zones and there will be a Cardinal, a Fixed, and a Mutable energy field assigned to each zone.

Physics would say that Cardinal signs are like centrifugal force, meaning their energies emanate quickly from the center of a circle. They shoot outward in an initiating manner. Cardinal signs have a tendency to stir things up and shake up the status quo. They ask us to go beyond our comfort areas.

Fixed signs are similar to centripetal force, meaning they send energy back toward the center of a circle. These signs tend to compress energy. They are stabilizing and have a maintaining quality. These are very determined signs that show us wanting things on our own terms.

Finally there are Mutable signs, which are like wave motion in physics that transports energy from one place to another. Mutable signs encourage us to be adaptable and flexible. They point us toward anticipating change and preparing for the future.

The four seasons are another way to explain the energy of Cardinal, Fixed, and Mutable sign energy. Cardinal signs launch or mark the beginning of the new seasons: Cardinal Aries introduces spring, Cardinal Cancer starts summer, Cardinal Libra brings fall, and Cardinal Capricorn starts winter. A Fixed sign immediately follows each Cardinal one. These signs deepen our experience of each season. Taurus follows Aries, Leo follows Cancer, Scorpio follows Libra, and Aquarius follows Capricorn. The Mutable signs prepare us for the end of a season and the start of a new one. They signal a changing of the guard. Gemini follows Taurus, Virgo follows Leo, Sagittarius follows Scorpio, and Pisces follows Aquarius. The Cardinal signs bring the equinoxes and solstices, the Fixed signs maintain a season, and the Mutable signs take us into a transition of one season into the next.

The past-life patterns for your sign are based just as much on your corresponding zone sign ruler for your day of birth as much as your Sun sign. In other words, if you were born a Leo and are in the Second Zone, ruled by Sagittarius, both Leo and Sagittarius went into the formula for tracing your past-life patterns. It's the combination of both signs that symbolizes your past-life patterns. Once again, if you were born in the First Zone of a sign, you will have the same sign repeating as your zone ruler. You will be a "double" in this sign and this is what was used to identify your past-life patterns.

The Twelve Astrological Signs: Ambassadors of the Collective Unconscious

It might sound strange to think of yourself as a mixture of the twelve signs, but we will be asked by the universe to understand the basic nature of each sign over the span of a lifetime. Why? Because the twelve signs encompass the complete experience in which your soul needs to be immersed. It is true you were born under a particular Sun sign and in a sign zone as described in this book. This does put a special emphasis on that particular sign as a way for you to shine.

Carl Jung coined the term *Collective Unconscious*. He explained that each of us has a conscious mind to use for immediate perceptions. Our conscious mind is made up of our personal nature. In addition, Jung said we have a personal unconscious mind made up of our memories from this lifetime. Some of these memories may have been forgotten or repressed and thus are no longer in our conscious awareness. What then did he mean by the Collective Unconscious? Well, this is where it all gets very interesting for you and me!

The Collective Unconscious is a vast reservoir of information independent of our memory. It is similar in nature to the concept known as the *akashic record*. The akasha is considered a library or universal memory bank containing all of the thoughts and events that have ever occurred since the beginning of time. It has been described as a universal computer that is constantly being updated. It is believed that the famous psychic Edgar Cayce had a natural ability to tune into this vast energy system. People with clairvoyant ability have an unusual capacity to tap into the sacred worlds of the akashic record and the Collective Unconscious.

The Collective Unconscious existed before we were even born. This is a collection of *symbols* shared by all of humanity, a product of ancestral experience from all civilizations since the beginning of time. Jung further explained that the Collective Unconscious does not develop individually. Then where does it have its origin? According to Jung, this vast energy system is inherited by each of us. The Collective Unconscious therefore is composed of preexisting forms. Jung named these forms *archetypes*. He said as we grow in awareness, we will become conscious of these original inherited patterns, or forms of thought and experiences. Our consciousness can expand through things like dreams, insight, and exploring metaphysical subjects. In essence, archetypes are the ancient, unconscious source of what we think and believe as people. Although there are collective interpretations of the symbols in differing cultures, we have the freedom to interpret their meaning for our own lives.

The twelve signs of the zodiac are symbols that have their own birth in the Collective Unconscious. Think of them as having archetypal meaning. Perhaps it will sound unusual to consider the signs in this way. The signs offer ways for you to tune into their creative messages. As you read through the various chapters of the book, you may identify with a sign other than the sign you were born under; that's because part of your consciousness is greatly attuned to the energy frequency of other signs as well as your birth sign.

How to Utilize This Book

The sign chapters are designed to give you greater insight into your past-life tendencies. You might enjoy reading your own sign information or that of someone else you know. The discussions cover past-life tendencies associated with each sign. As you will see, there is no perfect sign, and each has its ups and downs. There is *light*, or places we use a sign influence consciously and clearly, as though we have learned the lessons it contains; and there is *shadow*, which points to the lessons we have yet to learn. Shadow is not necessarily negative, it just points to a part of ourselves that is hidden or repressed, waiting for us to discover it. Shadow material can become a powerful part of your creative self-expression when you learn how to integrate it productively into everyday life.

It is likely that you will intuitively feel a pull to read another sign's section. Think of it as synchronicity, or a meaningful coincidence! It is as though that sign is calling you to read it now, and that is how this book really works. To the seeker of greater truth, and even to an open-minded scientific thinker, intuition can lead you toward greater enlightenment. Listening to your intuition, that wonderful inner voice, will guide you toward applying the information in this book to your life. You can simply go to your own sign chapter to gain a more personal reading, or you may open the book to any page and see if it speaks to you!

As previously stated, we are more than just our Sun sign. Some readers will know their birth chart and will want to read the chapters for those signs that are accentuated in their chart. What if you have never had your chart done by a professional astrologer? That's okay. Let your intuition guide you to the sections you are meant to read. What you need to read will call out to you.

Ordering Your Own Astrological Chart

If you would like to have your own astrology chart, go to my website for instructions on how to do so: www.bernieashman.com. You will be shown the best way to get this done.

Aries: The Warrior

3/21-4/19

Traditional Astrology Phrase: "I Am"
Archetypal Theme: Self-Expressive Embodiment

First Zone of Aries: **3/21–3/30**
Element: **Fire**
First Zone Sign Ruler: **Aries**
First Zone Energy Field: **Cardinal**
First Zone Signs: **Aries plus Aries = Bold Action**

Current Life Scan for the Aries First Zone

Your soul could not wait to get here to get the show started! What reveals this? You were born in the First Zone of Aries. Having your entrance into this life through this First Zone of Aries shows you to have relentless energy. Future goals are exhilarating to your mind. Your self-starting mode ignites spontaneously. There is no time for boredom, is there? Others may admire your tendency to leap forward and not worry about the consequences until later.

Your competitive spirit is contagious. Courage often comes after you overcome the fear of taking on a new challenge. Or maybe it's better to say you dare yourself into facing down what scares you. Leadership roles are your reward when you prove that you can channel your energy productively and responsibly. You do enjoy having plenty of latitude to call your own shots.

Your fiery personality likes to blaze new trails. You get more accomplished when learning how to pace yourself. Communicating your plans to others and listening to their needs wins their cooperation. *A primary drive is clarifying your true identity.* If you take the time to tune into your deepest thoughts, you will see that many of your actions are performed to secure a clearer sense of your true self.

Past-Life Patterns for the Aries First Zone

The past-life issues for you were associated with two key themes. One was *assertion*. You will notice the past-life patterns were linked to either being too assertive or not being assertive enough. Another theme was *lacking patience and insight* when moving too fast. This doesn't mean you were always this way. It's only saying you weren't as successful in your life when overindulging in these behaviors. It's typical of Aries First Zone past-life patterns to involve speed. You had a tendency to move at the speed of light, and probably still do!

Throwing Caution to the Wind

You got into trouble when you didn't pay attention to limits. Your deep desire to conquer obstacles sometimes kept you too much in the fast lane. Not paying attention to the signals that were telling you to slow down made you suffer the consequences. Your warrior instincts helped you to be successful in fighting your enemies. It's when you didn't take the time to pause and think about the consequences of your actions that you ended up taking one step forward and three steps back. People admired your ferocious energy but didn't always appreciate the way you neglected their own needs.

Battering Ram

You have a long history of being blessed with primeval survival instincts. Your First Zone birth points to this. This wasn't necessarily a bad thing. In past incarnations, it only resulted in negative results when you took it to the extreme. Being too forceful was the problem. This pattern often had its roots in your fear. When you tried to hide your insecurity is when you pulled out this weapon, and it may have won you a few battles but cost you the war. You alienated those trying to understand your inner motivations. Running away from your fears only made those fears stronger. This behavior was a defense mechanism used to insulate you from feeling anything.

Hiding Behind a Macho Persona

This pattern was related to identity and assertion. You were a master at hiding behind a persona or mask that was not the real you. Each of us does this to some extent; it's only when you overly identified with the outer world that you got really confused. It was when you would not let those close to you see who you really were that life got difficult, and sometimes downright lonely. A refusal to drop your shield of pretense sometimes led you down a road of inner turmoil.

Becoming too merged with a career to the point of thinking it was your entire identity caused you to become lost. You tried too hard in some incarnations to display a false sense of strength. It kept others at a distance. A lack of trust played into this pattern.

Low-Level Intensity

This may sound like a contradiction to a First Zone pattern, but it isn't. If this description seems more like you now, then it could be a carryover theme from past lives where you were underassertive. Holding back your directness kept your energy bottled up. This points to a fear of expressing your boldest ideas and getting your needs fulfilled. Denying your own goals kept you disoriented. You surrendered your power too easily. Trying to please people to the extreme got you into limiting life circumstances. Settling for being less than you could be only held you back from opportunities.

Illumination for the Current Life

If these Aries First Zone patterns are still active in this life, there are ways to turn them into positive allies. Your sign is capable of brave action. It sometimes only takes a little tweaking of a pattern to get it to change. Then again, if it is deep-seated, it will take a lot of practice to alter your thinking to a more fulfilling approach.

In the Throwing Caution to the Wind pattern, a little reality-testing before you take that leap into the unknown will get you better results. If you are thinking you need to prove you have the strength to succeed, you may be trying too hard. You thrive on competition; it's in the bones of an Aries person like yourself. Knowing your limits will make for a happier life. People will trust you more when they see you exercising sound judgment. The aftermath of taking reckless chances may leave your life in an endless state of flux. It's amazing how much more you will get back for the energy you expend if you take more time to calculate the best options for yourself.

To solve the Battering Ram pattern, you need to seek a balance of power in your negotiations. When you try to overpower others, you put them on the defensive. People will oppose you rather than be your friends. Seeking win-win situations is better than feeling you must conquer at all costs. If you realistically assess your life, you will see that you tend to lose what you want to achieve by forcing your demands on others. A teaspoon of humility goes far in turning an enemy into an ally. Hidden anger that you haven't faced might be the source of this pattern. Learn to express your feelings more openly. It could be the remedy to heal old wounds that are causing you to act with extreme force. If you acknowledge your fears, they have less power over you. This will keep you from being explosive. When you tune into this powerful energy, it will begin to work more for you than against you. It will even be more possible to channel this dynamic energy creatively into your work and other pursuits. Your relationships will be easier to manage and enjoy. There is a large payoff if you bring this past-life behavior into clear expression.

The Hiding Behind a Macho Persona pattern means you need to come out from behind the mask and show others who you really are. Why? There is more than one reason. First, letting people see the real you improves your romantic and professional possibilities. The people you want to impress find it easier to connect with you. They don't have to break down walls or get through the barriers between you and them. It makes for smoother sailing in all of your personal relations. Second, dropping the mask releases your greatest creative power. You probably don't realize how much of your energy gets siphoned off in concealing your identity. It is draining to portray false pretenses. It's like being an actor in a play but you aren't sure of your part. You can't give your all because you can't get into the role, because it's not the real you. By hiding your true identity, you are indulging in behavior that blocks your perceptions. It certainly confuses those trying to get to know you on deeper levels. You go through a wonderful rebirth when embracing your true self. The rebirth flies even higher when you let the world see a truer picture of you. A magical reinventing of your creative processes kicks into gear when you allow this metamorphosis to occur. Expressing the real you takes some Aries courage, which came packaged in you at birth. So you see, it's a small step to reaching out and accomplishing this change.

The Low-Level Intensity that runs contradictory to your fiery Aries nature is a past-life pattern that is neutralized through learning how to trust your intuition. You are likely a very sensitive person. Perhaps you try too hard to please others. Being more assertive is required in order to get your own needs met. You may need more equality in your relationships. When you reclaim your power, you will feel more complete; when you don't, a part of you feels like it's missing. If you deny your own power, you might attract individuals that are happy to take control of your life. This pattern can keep you stuck in dead-end situations. Experiencing your own intensity means you can tune into deeper parts of your creative power. Taking the risk to express your ideas directly frees you from this pattern. In not fearing the rejection of your opinions, you transcend this limiting behavior. Your passion to be yourself attracts the support you need from the world. You will find doors opening that previously remained closed. By more forcefully living out your positive thinking, you create a different world of options for yourself. Being born in this First Zone means you have the innate power to change your life. It only takes a little practice at getting more confident. The reward for overcoming this pattern is liberation from people, places, and circumstances that were in the way of realizing your greatest potential.

RoadMap to Your Empowerment

The First Zone of Aries is a climate for initiating action. It is a hot spot for acting on impulse. Being born in this First Zone means you have plenty of energy to tap into. *The key to your personal empowerment is in knowing how to stay cool in the midst of moving very fast.* Learning how to slow down just enough to take in all of the scenery is vital to your happiness. When you don't pace yourself, you could leave behind something needed for success. You are fortunate to be blessed with so much creative passion. The challenge is finding out how to master the intense energy running through your mind. Physical exercise can help.

Learning mind-centering techniques could be a valuable aid in getting the most mileage out of your natural gifts. Steadying your mind in the middle of a crisis helps you make the right decisions. Taking the time to think ahead to your next move before taking action saves you time, money, and energy.

Are you lacking the momentum needed to make changes and just don't feel assertive enough? Then it's important to find ways to catapult yourself out of what is keeping you stuck. First Aries Zone individuals like you get very frustrated when they can't get moving toward their goals. The gravitational push of this high octane First Zone is naturally enticing you to move forward. You only need to find the right emotional support and pragmatic wisdom to ignite you. You need to awaken your consciousness to reclaim your power! You might need to be a little more self-focused than in the past to balance your own needs with what others are expecting from you. Give yourself permission to be rewarded and to be the center of attention.

Develop awareness about your impact on others when trying to negotiate with them. You may not always be conscious of how you are too intense in getting what you want. Try to be more inclusive of the needs of others when making decisions or embarking on a course of action. Remember you are operating from a high-energy First Zone!

Second Zone of Aries: **3/31–4/9**
Element: **Fire**
Second Zone Sign Ruler: **Leo**
Second Zone Energy Field: **Fixed**
Second Zone Signs: **Aries plus Leo = Creative Passion**

Current Life Scan for the Aries Second Zone

Your soul was very motivated to get into the play of life and start experimenting with creative expression. You wanted independence early so you could start making your own mark on life. Being born in the Second Zone of Aries drives you to find plenty of outlets for a mind that is on fire to explore uncharted territory. You enjoy being a trendsetter and hearing the applause from others for your know-how.

People appreciate your belief in them. You are a natural cheerleader. You like to lead by example, which either makes others like you or envy you. Your desire to begin new projects is intense. You finish what you are passionate about and tend to leave undone what begins to bore you. Your business sense is sharp. Risk taking either pays big dividends or ends up as a big life lesson when you lose. You like to shower those you love with attention and are hurt easily when they don't return the affection.

Being a Fire sign, you move fast but tend to really slow down and focus on your serious ambitions. You prefer life on your own terms, as this is a Fixed energy zone, and don't like making too many concessions. *A primary drive is tuning into a deeper sense of your identity through your creative accomplishments.* When you include those you love in making the big decisions, they feel better about trusting you. When you learn how to compromise with a lover, you begin to create a special relationship. Your commitment to excellence is without rival. Leadership roles sometimes showcase your work ability. When you relax into your life, your mental outlook tends to be more positive.

Past-Life Patterns for the Aries Second Zone

The past-life issues for you were connected to two key themes. One was the *use of power*. You will notice that the past-life patterns were associated with either overpowering others or not claiming enough power. Another area was an extreme *self-orientation*. This doesn't mean you constantly used these behaviors, but only that you lost your way when they grew too dominant. It's typical of Aries Second Zone past-life patterns to involve restlessness. You had a tendency to require a lot on your plate to keep your mind occupied, and likely still do in this incarnation!

Need for Constant Action

You were a restless soul. Boredom was an enemy and you ran from it, sometimes to the point of exhaustion. You possessed a Type A energy system long before the term was coined in modern times. Roots did not form easily in some lives. You rebelled against stability. It was a habit to create friction just for the sake of friction. This drive to fight against harmony and peace was an adrenaline rush. You felt like you were in a race against time. Getting grounded was a tough challenge. You couldn't slow yourself down. You often didn't finish what you started.

Fixed Agendas

In some lives you were stubbornly attached to your own plans, to the point of not being able to compromise. Power struggles were common due to your unyielding positions on ideas. Your passion for winning and being viewed as right often put you at odds with others. A bossy attitude created friction in your business dealings as well as in your romantic relationships. You often had wealth, but it didn't necessarily bring you happiness. Finding closeness was a struggle because you felt a need to be in control at all times. You found the going easier when you were able to share the stage; when your need for attention was extreme, you were not as much fun to be close to.

Me First

There were past lives when you were too demanding of being number one at all times. It put others on the defensive. You had a strong drive to get ahead. It served you well in the professional world, but it didn't make people like you when you were compulsively after the winner's circle. Desiring success is not what threw your life out of balance; it was craving that the spotlight be constantly on you that caused friction with those you loved and at times in business dealings. When you did not pay attention to the needs of others, you were not popular. Your accomplishments got noticed in a big way. You sometimes got too attached to the applause and felt less important if you didn't get great recognition for your talents.

Dump Truck

This theme might not seem like it belongs in this Second Zone of Aries, but it does. There were past lives where you had trouble being extroverted. You were downright introverted! Your emotions and anger got bottled up. You became explosive if you held back your feelings too long. In other words, all of your anger came out all at once. You tended to dump your anger in one big bang. You took out your bad moods on people who were not even the source of your irritation. Instead of being more outspoken with those who were squashing your rights and goals, you unleashed your anger on whoever was in your path. This hurt those you loved and didn't make you feel any better after you vented pent-up emotions.

Illumination for the Current Life

If any of the past-life patterns of the Aries Second Zone are still a recurring problem in the current life, there are ways to overcome them. You will need to reach for some of that Aries courage and take a bold new step. It's okay if it's a small step—it does require practice and patience to change old patterns.

In Need for Constant Action, you only need to refocus yourself. Learning how to slow down will take some definite determination.

You will find that you will get more accomplished when you have a strategy rather than moving forward with no plan. The good news is that you have plenty of stabilizing energy by being born in the Aries Second Zone. There is actually much staying power embedded in this Fixed-energy zone, but you may need to dig deeper to tap into it. This zone responds better when you prove you can take the heat in the kitchen, as the old saying goes. You really need to step up to the plate! The ruling sign of your Second Zone, Leo, shows that when you discover your true creative passion, you can reach high levels of self-mastery. You need to find life pursuits that are interesting enough to capture your attention. This is really the trick in getting the most mileage out of your energy. When you conquer a fear of following through on a goal to its completion, your self-esteem gets a lift to a higher level.

To make the Fixed Agendas disappear as a pattern in this life, it is going to take some new programming of your mind. You will need to loosen your grip and see that it is more energizing not to always need to be in control. Your mind is working overtime when pushing your agenda to the exclusion of listening to others. Power struggles take a constant focus of your mental processes, but that focus is in the wrong direction. You actually benefit from compromising. Why is this so? You will find people are less resistant when they perceive you to be tolerant of their point of view. They want to cooperate rather than fight. Your love relationships and professional connections flow better when you adopt a more open attitude. Your health gets a boost because you are not experiencing as much stress. Your mind, body, and spirit are in harmony when you rise above this past-life nemesis.

The Me First pattern is neutralized by sharing the stage rather than pushing the other actors out of the way. You are fortunate to have a great deal of ego strength and determination by being a Second Zone person. That's a good thing. When you pay attention to what others need, your life gets into balance. When you are perceived as an empowering agent and a force of good in someone's life, it helps lessen the impact of this pattern, making it a distant memory. When you are less concerned about being the center of attention and simply let your talent do your talking, the world embraces you. This Second Zone pushes you to seek new opportunities. When your awareness grows to the point of seeing that the playing field of life is a large enough platform for you as well as for others, you'll find an endless number of opportunities appear. Developing keener insight is the key to rising above the hold of this pattern.

The Dump Truck stays out of this current life if you learn how to be more expressive of your feelings. You don't need to fear your anger. Anger is a natural emotion, and the experts say anger is really just hurt feelings. When you hold back your emotions until they reach a boiling point, eventually they will explode. Tuning into your moods might be one way to get a read on your anger. Learning to trust those you love enough to directly express your feelings really helps lessen the intensity of this pattern. Talking, believe it or not, is the best way to heal this behavior. The more you stay quiet, the more you are empowering the problem. Even small disagreements grow out of proportion when you hold back your emotions. It starts to convolute your perceptions. The fog will clear when you are bold enough to say what's on your mind.

RoadMap to Your Empowerment

The Second Zone of Aries is an exciting region, as it can feel like a continuous rebirth of creative energy. Being born in this zone means you feel younger when you are inspired. *The key to your personal empowerment is developing objectivity.* Balancing your own needs with those of others makes for greater harmony in this life. You have the capacity to motivate people to be all they can be. Your self-confidence takes you far. You feel more at ease when discovering your talents and allowing the world to see them.

When you find a relaxed ease within yourself, your actions become more focused. There is no need to impress others but simply to further master your skills. Sharing love instead of demanding it is the path to greater happiness. It's better that others don't fear you because it takes the tension out of your negotiations. Power struggles are infrequent when you are honest about your true motives. It's okay to be competitive; you just need to be harder on the problems than you are on people.

Expressing feelings openly keeps others from having to guess what's on your mind. In communicating more directly, you will hold less of your emotions inside. Angry outbursts are less likely if you make your thoughts visible. Getting past the fear of saying what you feel opens many avenues to creative possibilities. Your romantic, family, and professional aspirations are easier to realize when you don't hide your feelings.

Third Zone of Aries: **4/10–4/19**
Element: **Fire**
Third Zone Sign Ruler: **Sagittarius**
Third Zone Energy Field: **Mutable**
Third Zone Signs: **Aries plus Sagittarius = Variety Is the Spice of Life**

Current Life Scan for the Aries Third Zone

Your soul felt the calling to come into this life with a renewed spirit to
explore every possible angle toward self-discovery. Being born in the
Third Zone of Aries fills you with a natural instinct to communicate
and share knowledge. Being a teacher and advisor is always at your
fingertips. An inner restlessness to travel mentally and physically is
often displayed. New experiences keep you feeling alive and well.

When you feel inspired, the cup of life seems more than half full,
but you lose your zest when you have no goals. There must be a purpose or mission to keep you motivated. You are more idealistic than
the other Aries zones. Seeking a soul mate is heartfelt. You came into
this incarnation with a longing to have a partner and traveling com-
panion on many levels. Your ideals may need some reality-testing from
time to time, but without them you are like a fish out of water.

You like to know you have options before committing to long-
range goals. When people try to pressure you into making decisions,
you rebel. Freedom is your mantra. But you do feel a strong desire to
have a peaceful home to return to and even someone lovable to share
the experience. Partnerships stimulate you, and friends from all walks
of life are preferred. You respect those who walk their talk. You have
a yearning to be understood. You enjoy broadcasting your most cherished beliefs so that others might be motivated to join you in a lively
debate. *A primary drive is finding expansive life pursuits that keep you
growing.*

Past-Life Patterns for the Aries Third Zone

The past-life issues for you were linked to three themes. One was *overconfidence* based on false assumptions. You didn't feel like you could lose even though the odds were stacked against you. A second trend was a *loss of faith* in your abilities, which was pure poison to your momentum and threw your timing of major changes out of sync. A third trend was *judging others* too harshly, which caused problems in your relationships. You have a long history of past lives displaying a deep desire to live out your highest ideals. You truly believed the truth would set you free.

Fools Rush in Where Angels Fear to Tread

This typifies a pattern that has probably followed you from one incarnation to another. There were past lives that found you not scaring so easily. You liked the adrenaline rush of impulsively entering high-risk situations, but problems arose when you lost a lot more than you won. Your romantic relationships started fast and often ended even faster. You did not listen to the advice of friends who tried to get you to slow down before taking such extreme chances. Emotional and financial losses were the end result when you refused to assess circumstances ahead of time. You relied more on luck than logic. Learning from past mistakes was not your top priority, so you continued to repeat the same errors in judgment. You were brilliant but didn't listen to the voice in your head that was trying to tell you not to open the door to disaster. The underlying cause of this behavior was running away from yourself.

Rush to Judgment

When you became too attached to your own viewpoints, there was a tendency to indulge in this behavior. You argued endlessly, hoping to tire those not agreeing with you. The strategy was to get people to surrender to your opinions by never compromising. You had a fast mind that impulsively latched onto an immediate decision. This made you think your perspective was the only possible way to see a situation. This did cause real struggles in your relationships and business life.

Rather than stepping back to objectively think through your thoughts, you tended to jump right on a fast track, pushing for your own views. You exhausted yourself in marathon verbal disputes and angered those who were trying to be your friends.

Missing the Boat

A loss of faith in your abilities resulted in this pattern. You were at a standstill if you couldn't be driven by great self-confidence. Belief in your values and ideals fueled your engine; when this belief took a big dip, you were stopped in your tracks. The result was missed opportunities. A lack of assertion caused you to walk in circles. You felt like you were building bridges that led to nowhere. Your emotional confusion usually got in the way of mental clarity, stifling your actions. Sometimes this pattern became activated when you were disappointed by those you believed in. Extreme romantic setbacks took the wind out of your sails. Another cause of this pattern was a great sensitivity to criticism from those you loved or respected. If the criticism grew too extreme, it blocked you from moving forward.

Lost Passion

This one may be hard for you to imagine for you. When you thought you were not perfect enough, you would not take the first step toward a goal. Your thwarted search for the "perfect" romantic partner sometimes caused you to hold back your passion. The search for the "perfect" career held you back because there really was no such thing, and still isn't! Your passion was weakened when you lacked self-confidence. Your assertion was not getting the push you needed due to low self-esteem. You had a powerful creative passion that wasn't being ignited.

Illumination for the Current Life

If these past-life patterns are manifesting again in this life, there are ways to counteract them. It does take constant diligence to reverse the impact of a pattern. If you stick to it, you can overcome any of these past-life issues.

For the Fools Rush in Where Angels Fear to Tread pattern, you will need to adopt a new reality-testing strategy. You will be quite pleased when you break the hold of this pattern. Why? Because your actions will bring better results. You won't have to waste so much time pursuing paths that have no chance for success. Your relationships and business aspirations will be more balanced, and you can have the harmony and happiness that's been missing. Your lovers will be on the same page and team with you. Your professional satisfaction will be more solid and profitable. Your emotions won't be riding on a roller coaster that drains you. When you truly face yourself and stop running away from reality, the payoff is great. It's okay to take calculated risks. Taking your time and pursuing better-planned goals is wise. Your identity gets clearer when you stay away from temptations that are not in your best interest. If you get bored easily, try finding better choices for the excitement you need. Fill your mind with growth-promoting information and avoid situations that detract from your personal fulfillment.

In Rush to Judgment, you will need to broaden your perspective and be more tolerant of differing opinions. If you agree to disagree, many potential arguments can be avoided. You benefit greatly when allowing for freer exchanges of information. If you become a better listener, you will find others more agreeable to your needs. Your family, romantic, and professional relationships become more flowing. People will tend to cooperate more when they see you are listening to their ideas. If you process information rather than react too quickly, you find there will be less to argue about. You will lose less energy in verbal disputes when you open your mind to opposing views.

The Missing the Boat pattern might require a renewed faith. You are lost when you don't believe in your future goals. Tuning into why you are lacking assertiveness is essential. It could be that you need to break free from overly critical individuals who negate your goals. If you have a fear of taking a risk, you may need to try the Swiss cheese theory (taking small steps at a time to complete a plan). If you focus too much on the whole picture, it may be discouraging. Sometimes you only need to take that painful first step to find it isn't that hard to get going. There can be a need to trust your instincts. You won't know unless you take a leap of faith. It's okay to make a mistake. It's better to get moving because the momentum could be what it requires to take advantage of an opportunity.

To keep Lost Passion in check, you will need to not try to be so perfect. You have too much intensity to sit on it for long, don't you agree? Let go and don't be afraid to make a mistake. Being born in this Aries Third Zone shows you have plenty of knowledge to figure your way out of just about anything. Let that fire ignite! You do better when making your move forward toward a desired result. You might need to visualize the result with a lot of positive thinking and then move. Realize that there are no perfect people, so don't have unrealistic expectations of yourself. Also, don't expect to find a perfect partner in life. You have more fun when you have realistic goals. Even careers are not perfect. Ambition is fine, but there is no need to put this much pressure on yourself. There is a work niche just right for you. It might take a little experimentation to pin this down. Let people see your talent—it opens the door for opportunity. Your emotions run deep, so let your intuition guide you to higher plateaus.

RoadMap to Your Empowerment

The Third Zone of Aries is a vast oasis for gaining new knowledge with the sign Sagittarius as the sign zone ruler. It has an eclectic atmosphere that stimulates you to draw learning from a wide variety of experiences. Being born in this adventurous region encourages you to explore many subjects. *The key to your personal empowerment is having faith in your ability and learning how to stay focused.* You came into this life to have an open mind. You will stay invigorated through a continuous appreciation for new information.

Enthusiasm is an important ingredient to your everyday success. You are goal-oriented. You are at your best when you have faith in the future. It's vital that your closest allies in life have a positive outlook. You are impressionable and sensitive in this Aries Third Zone. Your ideals and values are the fire that keeps you motivated. People will often look to you for advice. Writing and teaching may become part of your self-expression in a big way. Remember to keep a very open mind in your communication. It's your ticket to highways of opportunity!

Taurus: The Builder

4/20-5/20

Traditional Astrology Phrase: "I Have"
Archetypal Theme: Desire for Comfort & Beauty

First Zone of Taurus: **4/20–4/29**
Element: **Earth**
First Zone Sign Ruler: **Taurus**
First Zone Energy Field: **Fixed**
First Zone Signs: **Taurus plus Taurus = Immense Persistence**

Current Life Scan for the Taurus First Zone

Your soul craved a chance to explore and taste the sensual pleasures of the world. What indicates this? You were born in this Taurus First Zone! This is a relaxing region filled with a love of beauty and physical pleasure. There is a deep desire to find stability and peace as well. You are blessed with patience. Others may sometimes wish you did not wait so long before taking action. The trick is getting yourself motivated toward a reward that sets your wheels in motion.

Being from a Fixed zone energy, you prefer having things on your own terms. That's okay as long as you don't go overboard in always having to get your own way. You win more friends with a give-and-take attitude. When people sense you are a team player, they tend to be more cooperative.

Your earthy way of being pragmatic in planning your goals helps you finish what you start. It's a side of you people can admire. *A primary drive is developing a healthy self-esteem*. It's the key to unlocking the doors to your happiness. Somewhere deep in your consciousness you already know this, don't you? When you value yourself, you find it easier to find contentment and a sense of ease in your everyday life.

Past-Life Patterns for the Taurus First Zone

The past-life issues for you moved along three paths. One was the *pleasure principle*, or overindulging in the finer things of life. Another was a *strong stubborn streak*. You weren't always this way but did have a tendency to lean in this direction in getting what you wanted. It's not so unusual for Taurus First Zone patterns to be tied to firmly standing your ground. It's more like standing in cement! You were in the habit of locking onto certain attitudes. A final theme was *low self-esteem*— perhaps the most troublesome theme when it became a dominant force in an incarnation.

Aphrodisiac

You lost your way in past lives when you became too attached to things that took you off center. There was a tendency to love pleasure to the extreme. It was problematic when you became addicted to people or substances, and your emotional and mental well-being suffered the consequences. In some past incarnations, you tried to escape your problems through romantic relationships. You too often got into partnerships that lacked balance. The fulfillment you were seeking did not materialize because you were running away from your problems. You lost out on more satisfying experiences of love, abundance, and creative success.

Bullheaded

It may not come as a surprise that you were accused of being stubborn in past lives. This is a pattern that may have followed you into this lifetime. Because this is a Taurus-Taurus zone, you have an extra dose of wanting things on your own terms. This is part of a long history of being ruggedly determined to get your own way. It sometimes led you to great success, but at the same time caused tension with those you loved. Power struggles were a regular occurrence. A dogged persistence to push your own ideas without compromising did throw your life off-center.

All Dollars and No Sense

There were times in past lives when you got lost in material consciousness to the point of drowning out everything else. Ambition became too important, greatly outweighing the importance you placed on people. You stopped growing spiritually and displayed a strong focus on self to the exclusion of noticing what other people in your life needed. Your competitive drive helped you get ahead of others, but in the end you felt empty inside. Developing a broad life awareness or perspective was absent. You tended to grow sad and felt emotionally isolated in past lives when this desire for success became the sole object of your devotion.

Hole in Your Pocket

This pattern showed a compulsive desire to spend and buy with no plan for securing the future. In some lives this was caused by low self-esteem; you tried to fill an inner void by purchasing more and more things. It became troublesome when you didn't value your inner being enough. Your emotional confusion caused you to make impulsive decisions that yielded bad results. A tendency to take unnecessary risks didn't make for a stable life. Your momentum to finish what you started grew sluggish due to poor planning and a lack of motivation.

Illumination for the Current Life

If these Taurus First Zone patterns are still manifesting in your current life, there are ways to make them work in your favor. It might take regular effort to overcome their negative pull. Remember, it likely took several incarnations for these patterns to grow strong, so it might take your Taurus determination to quiet down their interference with your happiness. Think positively and anything is possible!

In the Aphrodisiac pattern, it's okay to have fun, but life is more harmonious for you when you don't run toward escapist behaviors. Redirecting your mental and emotional energies into more productive outlets is wise. It's actually the road back to your center. It could be that your expectations of yourself are too high. Sometimes an underlying theme in this pattern was unrealistic ideals. If you couldn't reach those high plateaus, you overindulged in things of this world that then took away from your power. So it's best to adopt more reasonable goals that really can be accomplished. Then the need to escape into self-defeating behaviors can disappear.

To counteract the Bullheaded pattern, you need flexibility. It is the lubricant that will keep you free of power struggles and gets people to be more cooperative. You will find more options will be available to you. There is no need to control everything; as a matter of fact, it's impossible to do so. It's great you have the determination and focus that comes standard when you are born in this Taurus First Zone; you only need to diversify your energy a bit. When you let others express their opinions openly, they feel valued in the way you seek to feel valued. So when you learn to accept new experiences and flow with some change, you can transcend this pattern.

With the All Dollars and No Sense pattern, you need to balance a strong, earthy, pragmatic mind with some intuitive experiences. You will prevent yourself from becoming a workaholic if you learn to indulge in other life endeavors. Your perceptions about life will deepen if you take a new approach to being a success. You can still work hard, but it's better to integrate a well-rounded learning attitude. You miss out on being with those you love when you spend all of your time worrying about profit, fame, and fortune. Changing your lifestyle might require an adjustment, but it will pay dividends you never imagined possible!

The Hole in Your Pocket pattern is reversible if you do things that build self-esteem. Sometimes it only takes a minor change in your thinking to make more positive circumstances a reality. An impulsive spending behavior can be replaced by seeking greater inner peace. It may require some inner reflection. You might need to leave a relationship or job that makes you feel impoverished. Rather than letting emotional confusion guide you, this takes a slower, steadier pace that really is a natural part of being born in this First Taurus Zone. You can tap into this wonderful energy through consciously making more constructive choices that solidify your inner being and point the way to harmony in your outer life.

RoadMap to Your Empowerment

The First Zone of Taurus is a fertile climate for creating a peaceful and rewarding life. It is a landscape providing an innate grasp of beauty. *The key to your personal empowerment is knowing when a change of scenery might be stimulating to your sense of well-being.* There is a strong drive to stay the course that comes with being born in this stability-oriented turf. Stopping to enjoy a view is fine, but remember to move forward because there is more to see and experience.

Do you sometimes feel like you are not moving fast enough? It could be that you need to rethink your game plan. A new job or project will sometimes make you feel brand-new. You like to feel needed; it is another natural influence of this First Taurus Zone. People likely perceive you as very resourceful. In many ways you are a doer, as seeing the results of your ideas and actions lifts your self-esteem to new heights. Having an active life with some variety keeps you thinking young and is good for your immune system.

Remember to accept change with a positive attitude. This doesn't mean you always have to compromise, but bending a little will get better results when negotiating. You have the potential to be good in art or music, and even the culinary world may be a place to display your creative talents. Having a natural instinct to make things or people appear more beautiful might be in your skill set. You feel better about yourself when you get a chance to showcase your work skills, and letting the world see your ability does wonders for your happiness and creative passion.

Second Zone of Taurus: **4/30–5/9**
Element: **Earth**
Second Zone Sign Ruler: **Virgo**
Second Zone Energy Field: **Mutable**
Second Zone Signs: **Taurus plus Virgo = Efficiency in Motion**

Current Life Scan for the Taurus Second Zone

Your soul looked forward to entering life with a well-conceived plan to make the best of each day on the earthly plane. Being born in the Second Zone of Taurus colors you with a sharp eye for business and a keen awareness of details. This is a Taurus region that causes you to be naturally attuned to learning better ways of getting a job done. It probably didn't take you long to find certain skills that defined you as a reliable worker.

There are times you probably wish you didn't worry so much about details. Then again, it's your constant attention to the little things many people ignore that opens up doors to success for you. You are self-driven, especially after finding self-confidence. When you are lucky enough to find a motivating teacher or leader to take you under their wing, there is no limit to how far you can go in life. You might need a little push to take a creative risk once in a while. If you are too humble, life could pass you by. It's when you trust your instincts that you break new ground. Learning to act on those intuitive hunches can give you a sense of renewal, spoken from that inner voice that tells you maybe this is an opportunity worth your time and energy.

Being an Earth sign—and especially one born in this particular zone—you are picky about your likes and dislikes. Your diet and health are important subjects of interest. You like people capable of making well-defined decisions. *A primary drive for you is being true to your highest ideals and acting on their inspiration.* This is what launches you into a world of wider landscapes. When you don't limit your options based on what others tell you isn't possible, the roads of opportunity and growth get much wider. You like making others feel better about themselves. It's in learning how to please both yourself and those you care about deeply that you find greater happiness.

Past-Life Patterns for the Taurus Second Zone

The past-life issues for you were linked to three areas, one being a *limited life perspective*. Another was a *negative outlook*. It's not so unusual for Taurus Second Zone past-life patterns to be connected to either seeing the cup as less than half full or not taking a broad enough perspective, which can be caused by playing it too safe. A third theme was a *nagging desire to be perfect*. This isn't saying that you were always operating this way. You did get off-track when these became very active themes in your past incarnations.

Extreme Earthbound Consciousness

When you lacked imagination or didn't ever take a risk, you had a tendency to get stuck in a rut. Habits in themselves were good things because they gave you a sense of order, but when you were afraid to try new things or experiment with new alternatives, you limited your options. You stayed in relationships, jobs, or places that didn't offer enough growth. You became too attached to doing the same thing, day after day and year after year. Your mind and spirit became dulled by a lack of stimulation. An overfondness for predictability destined you to limiting circumstances.

Poverty Consciousness

There were past incarnations that found you not believing enough in the power of abundance. Rather than believing that you deserved a rewarding life, your mind spent too much time on the other end of the spectrum. You attracted less than you could have due to focusing more on lack. This did cause you to not go after more progressive life directions. You had a solid understanding of frugality. You just couldn't bring yourself to get liberated from a mind-set that made you think the lucky breaks were only meant for others. Even the encouragement from close friends or family members did not talk you out of a fixed belief that you were not meant for greater success.

Inertia

There were times you seemed to simply stop in your tracks. You lost your momentum. Why? Sometimes it was not having a happy enough attitude. You got too worried about the details and talked yourself out of moving forward because you didn't think you could do something perfectly enough. There were times you tried too hard to be perfect for someone else or you had too-high expectations for others. In some past lives, this desire for perfection caused you to not compete at all. You lost your competitive edge in thinking you were not good enough to win.

Negative Addiction

When you paid too much attention to what might go wrong, you missed out on what might go right! Your left brain—that powerhouse of analysis and sifting through facts—sometimes got so strong that it overruled your intuitive right brain, which was trying to steer you away from worry to take you toward a more positive outlook. You actually had such a well-developed intellect that at times it worked against you. How? By keeping you too focused on trying to change what could not be changed. Instead of using your mind to find a better solution to your problems, you tended to dwell on why your obstacles could not be fixed. In other words, you resisted considering new roads to solutions.

Illumination for the Current Life

If the past-life patterns of the Taurus Second Zone are problematic in your current life, there are ways to get past them. It will take the steady effort your sign is known for in order to turn these negative energies into positive forces. If you make a conscious attempt to overcome these patterns, eventually their influence will lighten and one day be a distant memory.

The Extreme Earthbound Consciousness pattern requires that you mix things up a bit. Don't be afraid to try new things. Let go of the familiar. Contrast allows you to more objectively see if you are on the right path or not. Getting away from the same old routines refreshes your mind. It's a breath of needed fresh air when you travel to unfamiliar surroundings. Get out of those comfort zones and expand your mental borders. Let new experiences wash over you. New and stimulating learning experiences keep you young and alive. It's even good for your immune system to have more invigorating stimuli invade your everyday habits. Welcome new hobbies, books, movies, friends, and travel opportunities.

The Poverty Consciousness foe is converted into an ally by putting an end to desiring a lack of abundance. You may need to learn how to meditate, or at least start doing some positive affirmations that get you to focus on gaining wealth. You don't need to be the richest person in the world, but you do need to accept that you are worthy of being fairly compensated for your work. Your luck is better when you see that you deserve the good things in life. Greater success is possible if you have faith that you can accomplish your goals. First you need to have a positive approach toward your objectives. You will be pleased with the results and changes that can occur if you take on an upbeat mental outlook. If this seems like a difficult task, then take small steps. You may not change this pattern overnight. If you move with determination, life will reward you.

The Inertia pattern can be transcended by realizing that you don't need to try to be perfect. Give yourself a break! Imperfection is just part of life, and real life gets pretty messy. Even a thing that becomes a masterpiece did not begin as one. It's okay to make mistakes! It's how we learn, through trial and error. There are no perfect people, so don't expect to find any. You are better off when moving forward without paying too much attention to the details; you can always edit what you do later. When you put your creative intensity into what you do, it will guide you to your final destination. Learn to trust your intuition. There may be times when you will need a push from a friend or family member to get moving—let them help you. Don't hide your fear of taking on a new challenge. Share your concerns; talking about it might be just the key you need to unlock a new door.

The Negative Addiction pattern needs a huge injection of positive thinking to transform it. If you are still trapped by this pattern, it's probably been following you from one life into another for quite some time. Now it's time to make it disappear. You can do this by not keeping your mind glued to negative thoughts. It takes a lot of repetition in a new direction to climb to a high enough altitude to fly over this pattern. If a plan is not working, it doesn't do any good to obsessively think it can't get better. It's wiser to simply adopt a new strategy. Scrap the ones that don't work. Shred them! You have a powerful intellect—point it in a direction that gives a better option. Think in terms of alternatives. Think positively whether you need to take classes or read books to learn how to do so. You will have more mental and physical energy when you conquer this pattern.

RoadMap to Your Empowerment

The Second Zone of Taurus is a region that inspires you to be curious. Being born in this zone means you can walk through an endless number of new learning opportunities. *The key to your personal empowerment is nourishing your mind with positive thoughts.* When you do this, you are a person with a plan who can't be stopped.

Accepting your faults is just as vital to your happiness as being proud of your strengths. Giving yourself enough latitude to make errors takes the pressure off of you. It's wise to cut others some slack as well. You can't help trying to perfect your skills with meticulous Virgo as your zone sign ruler; just remember to be harder on the problems than on yourself or those you love.

Allow new stimulating experiences and people into your life. It's what keeps your soul, mind, and body moving forward smoothly. Don't stew in your worries, as this tends to wear you down. Let your ideals have as much influence as your intellect, and you will never stray too far off the road to harmony.

Third Zone of Taurus: **5/10–5/20**
Element: **Earth**
Third Zone Sign Ruler: **Capricorn**
Third Zone Energy Field: **Cardinal**
Third Zone Signs: **Taurus plus Capricorn = Maximizing Your Potential**

Current Life Scan for the Taurus Third Zone

Your soul looked forward with great anticipation to arriving onto the earth plane of consciousness. Why? Because much work was wanting to get accomplished on the mental, emotional, and spiritual levels! Being born in the Third Zone of Taurus accelerates your momentum to put what you value into practice. You really like to know where the rubber hits the road, meaning you like to define your reality clearly and get results.

This is one of the most ambitious sign zones. There is a deep desire to establish long, committed connections with people, and you expect others to give back to you the same loyalty that you give to them. Your romances, friendships, and group affiliations tend to be long-lasting. You respect traditions as long as they agree with your values. Feeling in control of your life means a lot to you. There is a natural ability to learn skills through experiencing them rather than through classroom training. Your focus is tremendous if you find work, goals, or projects that you ascertain as being worthy of your time. You detest people who waste your time.

You are often perceived as someone with a plan, whether you truly possess one or not. You like being well prepared before entering new challenges. Your confidence increases as you gain the knowledge to conquer new experiences. You really don't like defeat. *A primary drive is building a safe and reliable life that gains power with time.* Management instincts are readily at your fingertips. When you learn to flow with changing circumstances, you gain great wisdom. Letting your lovers and closest friends see the real you brings them closer.

Past-Life Patterns for the Taurus Third Zone

The past-life issues for you moved on three fronts. One was *extreme ambition drives*. Being number one was too important. However, another slant on this was incarnations where you lacked the will to claim your power. A second theme was *needing to be in complete control.* A third pattern was linked to an *excessive desire to only receive.* This isn't saying you were always exhibiting these behaviors. You did get off-course if you indulged in these ways of expressing yourself.

Desert Sands

There were past lives that featured a strong drive to get to the top of the success ladder. That in itself was not a problem. However, when you didn't care about anything but winning, you got into trouble. Emotional emptiness was the result—you alienated the very people you needed and depended on the most. In the end, your physical health suffered the consequences, as did your mental well-being. You grew depressed because you lacked an inner world that could sustain you through tough times. It was easy when you were on top but difficult when you started losing. Life has a way of dealing out ups as well as downs. When you really needed emotional and spiritual strength, it wasn't there. Your outer focus had all of your attention and your inner landscapes were as dry as a desert.

I Want to Rule You

You had incarnations that showed you needing to be in complete control of others. When you were hiding fears, this pattern became more visible. To compensate for your own inner uncertainty, you chose to be extra bossy. In other words, you were masking your anxiety about the present and future behind a false exterior of always being in control. This wasn't a fun way to live for you or for those close to you. Even when you had great wealth, there was still a temptation to act this way. You created power struggles by refusing to negotiate fairly. The desire to win at all costs drove you. There was little honest communication in your life when this pattern was too predominant.

Scrooge

In some incarnations, you believed in delayed gratification to the point of not rewarding yourself or others enough. Holding on to your money to the extreme deprived you of things that could have made you happy. This didn't make those closest to you feel appreciated. Your fears blocked you from taking advantage of the laws of abundance. If you gave more, you could have received more. There was a need to be in control at work in this pattern. You didn't like anyone else to have access to your resources. You were cautious to an extreme and not very trusting of others. You had a tendency to build walls around yourself, thinking this would make you invincible. The problem was that it kept you from sharing and caused great tension in your relationships.

Low Power Voltage

In this pattern you did not step up to the plate and declare your personal power. You lacked self-confidence. Sometimes this was due to trying too hard to please others; on other occasions, it was because you attracted power-hungry individuals who usurped all of the power in the partnership. Your assertiveness was near flat-line, meaning it was not very visible. You settled for a lot less than you could have had. Your relationships and jobs too often didn't give you a chance to discover the true you. Low self-esteem was the real issue here.

Illumination for the Current Life

If you are finding that these Taurus Third Zone patterns are manifesting in your current life, there are ways to get past them. It will take some of that gritty determination that comes standard in this zone to rise above their influences. Since the patterns may have been part of several past incarnations, you will need to be patient. Don't grow discouraged if it takes repeated practice to neutralize their impact.

In the Desert Sands pattern, you need to balance a strong drive for career success with taking care of the spiritual and emotional sides of life. Nobody is saying you should hold back your talents; just make sure you don't block all of the fun out of your life. Make time for play as well as work and you will be happier and healthier. When you go through challenges or setbacks, as we all do from time to time, you will have greater emotional strength to sustain you. It's important to pay attention to the people who love you. Their support is nice to have when you need it. Take part in a give-and-take with your closest allies. Developing outside interests beyond ambition adds greater meaning to your life.

To solve the I Want to Rule You pattern, you must relinquish your hold on the control button. It takes a lot of pressure off your mind when you let others be themselves. Letting your fear rule you is not wise. When you talk out your worries and include your friends and family in key decisions, you actually lighten your burden. Your mental and physical health gets a lift. If you want to rule your business world, maybe you should—but let others run their own world. It's best to have equality in your relationships. When you allow others to see where you are vulnerable, it can be scary at first, but you might be surprised and relieved to get a few things out in the open. Nobody is really happy having all of the power in a partnership. They may act that way but in their inner world is suffering and misery. So change your game plan. Hiding fear actually gives it power over you. Honest dialogue with your true friends makes for a tighter bond. When people fear you, they aren't really doing you any good. You are better off when others feel the freedom to talk honestly about what they expect and need from you. You will find the stimulation good when exchanging ideas openly. Even your career and ambition get energized!

In the Scrooge pattern, you need not keep such a tight lid on your resources. Trusting that the universe will replenish what you spend is the way to break free of this behavior. You need to have more faith in abundance. People will like you more if you share what you own and know. You are much happier when you reward yourself once in a while. When you hold back your money and possessions, people don't feel appreciated or loved, and they sense your lack of trust. Trust yourself more! Letting go a bit and enjoying the world is a good thing. Getting past your insecurity might take some effort, but it can be accomplished. Your energy levels may even improve by trusting that it's okay to spend some of what you have. You can stay on a budget if you like, but do yourself a favor and receive more of what life is trying to give you. How do you do this? It begins by more freely sharing yourself with others.

The Low Power Voltage rut is going to take some faith in yourself to get past. You may need to take some classes on assertiveness training or read books on the subject. You might have to be more selective about the types of people you let get close to you. Negative input from others is exactly what you don't need. If you have had years of being told you can't be your true self in this life, and you endured this in a few past incarnations, then it will take some time to reverse the pattern. But don't despair, you can change this around in your favor with real effort. You might need a life coach cheering you on or good friends doing this for you. Injecting doses of positive energy into your thinking does not hurt either! You can get the personal power meter registering much higher by simply refocusing your energy in new, positive directions that confirm a reinvented identity.

RoadMap to Your Empowerment

The Third Zone of Taurus is a wonderful climate for defining your ambitions clearly. Making a strong statement about your ability comes with a sense of ease when you find a clear internal strength. *The key to your personal empowerment is having faith that your dreams can come true without having to force them to occur.* Finding balance in your private and public lives gives you great self-assurance.

You learn from past experiences better than many. When you realize that your fears don't need to be the motivations behind your actions, you find true inner peace. Even your successes in the world come more smoothly. You attract abundance. Rather than trying to force life to respond to you, it's better when you find a flow. Being born in this very pragmatic and self-driven zone gives you plenty of passion for making your ideals a reality. Believing in the power of abundance is wise, as it sets you free. When you don't hold so tightly to what you own, the universe sends you plenty of gifts. When you take the time to notice the messages your intuitive voice is whispering to you, there are people and experiences waiting to greet you with open arms. Be generous to those deserving your support and they will return the favor.

Gemini: The Communicator

5/21-6/21

Traditional Astrology Phrase: "I Perceive"
Archetypal Theme: Conceptualization of Perception

First Zone of Gemini: **5/21–5/30**
Element: **Air**
First Zone Ruler: **Gemini**
First Zone Energy Field: **Mutable**
First Zone Signs: **Gemini plus Gemini = Fast Mental Impulses**

Current Life Scan for the Gemini First Zone

Your soul was anxious to explore life from many dimensions as soon as it landed! That's what being born in this First Gemini Zone indicates. You have one of the most curious minds in the world. It isn't necessarily easy for you to focus on one subject for an extended period of time unless it is of great interest to you. At least that's your general way of operating from day to day.

You make a great networker. Helping like-minded people make connections excites you. Exchanging ideas with others is exhilarating. You do need to watch out for overtaxing your mind with an endless number of details. However, it's hard for you to slow down when you are exploring your favorite interests. *A primary drive is a desire to stay mentally inspired.*

People lacking imagination probably bore you. You enjoy friends, coworkers, and lovers who are able to change directions in midstream, as you can. You possess an insatiable curiosity for information. There may not be one hobby or job that will completely satisfy your hunger for new knowledge, but you make a mighty fine teacher, consultant, writer, or advisor. Communication runs through your brain as smoothly as the Sun radiates light.

Past-Life Patterns for the Gemini First Zone

The past-life issues for you were connected to three themes. One was in *not knowing when to slow down*—the First Gemini Zone put the speed of light into your brain synapses and likely still does! Another theme was *purposely distorting facts.* A third dimension of your patterns was *jumping to erroneous conclusions*; fast mental impulses were at the root of some negative past-life patterns.

Dual Exhaustion

In some past incarnations, you didn't know when to put on the brakes when it came to ingesting information. You wore down your mind by not pacing yourself, and your mental and physical health suffered the consequences. A refusal to rest a very tired psyche got you into trouble. Your decisions sometimes lacked depth and clarity because you were making them from a sleep-deprived brain. People grew frustrated with you when your ideas and choices showed an extreme lack of logic, which could have been traced back to a weary mind. Running on empty energy caused you to occasionally enter relationships and jobs not best suited for you.

Forked Tongue

In this pattern, you purposely misled others to the point that they stopped trusting you. The fallout was that you didn't get to enjoy the close interpersonal communication you could have had. The underlying problem was often denial: you refused to acknowledge your behavior. You told yourself it was in your best interest to constantly distance yourself from others by not directly addressing information. You ran from conflict when it would have been better to deal with the issues in a direct manner.

Roadrunner

This rut—like the Dual Exhaustion pattern—involved moving too fast. You ran through life often not taking the time to smell the roses. Sometimes it was excessive ambition that fueled your mental fires; at other times it was simply that you thought you would miss out on something if you went at a slower pace. The fallout from this behavior was often that you left too much business unfinished. You expected others to fix the loose ends. This annoyed people and even frustrated you in that you didn't complete what you set out to accomplish.

Sarcastic Mouth

This pattern found you attacking others verbally. You had strong opinions, which in itself was not a bad thing. It was when you felt a burning passion to win an argument at all costs that you got into trouble. You had a problem seeing someone else's point of view. You became too dogmatic in pushing a cause or an idea. Hurt feelings didn't make others want to get to know you on a closer level. However, this was an okay trait in business, which was a different playing field than in your relationships and friendships. An unwillingness to let others have their fair say caused great tension in your personal interactions.

Illumination for the Current Life

If these Gemini First Zone patterns are problematic in this life, their influences can be conquered. There is a lot of mental ingenuity inherent in being born in this zone—if you stay at it, there is a great potential to be successful. It can take a lot of regular practice to overcome past patterns.

To transcend Dual Exhaustion, you need to concentrate more on the *quality* of information you seek rather than the *quantity*. You will find more energy by not trying to take in more than your brain can chew. Learn to rest your mind! It needs time to process what you have already absorbed. When you aren't experiencing so much fatigue, your perceptions are much sharper. Insight is really the key to keeping you on course and steering clear of relationships and work situations that don't allow you to be happy. Even your creative power intensifies when you aren't distracted by useless facts that you don't need to be successful.

The Forked Tongue pattern requires that you not try to hide your feelings. When you aren't sure of yourself is when you are most likely to fall back on this pattern. Denying that you are giving out misleading information can compound problems that already exist, so clearing the air with honest communication is a far better solution. The old saying "the truth will set you free" applies here. Running away from your differences of opinion takes you farther from solving a problem.

It's far better to negotiate openly with others. It is the best way to build trust and closeness.

Regarding the Roadrunner pattern, you need to sometimes make sure you pause. Why? Taking time to reflect keeps you from having to do things over again. If you take a little time to plan, you can find it easier to finish what you begin. People will be happier with you. When you learn how to focus your energy, your creative ability improves. There is nothing wrong with thinking and moving faster than others, just make sure you are maximizing your potential by not running in circles.

For the Sarcastic Mouth tendency, you must desire to accurately hear what someone else is saying. This means you need to be a better listener. There is no need to fight so ferociously all of the time to win every dispute. Choose your battles more wisely and you will be happier. You will enjoy your relationships if you allow others to speak freely. Try to create win-win situations. Your friends and lovers will come closer if you are tolerant of their ideas. It doesn't mean you have to always agree or say Yes when you mean No. If you are on the attack because you are hiding your fears, then come out from behind them. You will find life more enjoyable if you talk out your problems.

RoadMap to Your Empowerment

The First Zone of Gemini is a vast oasis for mental growth. It sends exhilarating impulses to learn skipping through your entire being. You might be the envy of many people when it comes to a rare ability to adapt quickly to change. When you focus your nervous energy productively, there is no end to how much you can accomplish. When you discover the life interests that capture your imagination, your inventiveness comes alive. *The key to your personal empowerment is having faith in your ability to determine the paths that will take you to a higher altitude from which to maintain mental clarity.*

Your ability to communicate has few rivals in other sign zones. You can excel in any field requiring communication skills. You like diversity and do need a lot on your plate to keep you happy. Your attention span wanes as you grow bored, so the more mentally invigorated you stay, the better. But do be careful not to become burned out due to filling your mind too quickly with information. You can get bombarded by too many stimuli.

Remember to try to talk directly when communicating. If you don't run from the truth, you will get what you really need from others rather than a lot of confusion. You feel greater clarity and power when you're able to accurately perceive reality.

Second Zone of Gemini: **5/31–6/10**
Element: **Air**
Second Zone Sign Ruler: **Libra**
Second Zone Energy Field: **Cardinal**
Second Zone Signs: **Gemini plus Libra = Social Excitation**

Current Life Scan for the Gemini Second Zone

Your soul was anticipating a wide range of social encounters as it embarked on its journey to get to this incarnation. Being born in this Second Gemini Zone with your sign zone ruler being Libra shows that, from the beginning, this was meant to be a life filled with a multitude of partnerships. You enjoy having a wide range of peers. You have a keen sense of knowing the right thing to say at the right time, which serves you well in business, romance, and other walks of life.

You probably prefer to get several opinions about a decision before finalizing it. There is a tendency to wait until the last minute before giving your final answer. People either appreciate your desire not to make impulsive choices or it frustrates them. You like individuals willing to cut you some slack rather than forcing you to move quickly.

Being an Air sign, you like people who are thinkers. If they have an aesthetic side or are true romantics, you may be especially attracted to them. *A primary drive is finding a sense of inner peace while at the same time creating a life script that keeps you mentally excited.* That might seem like a tall order, but being born in this imaginative Gemini Second Zone makes it possible to live in the best of both of these worlds!

Past-Life Patterns for the Gemini Second Zone

The past-life issues for you traveled along three distinct highways. One theme was trying to be what other people wanted you to be *rather than being yourself.* Another was *not letting others be themselves.* A third area was trying to move in too many directions at once, causing great *indecision.* You did not always exhibit these behaviors but lost your way when you did. You were a touch dramatic and probably still are a bit this way in this incarnation.

Double Messages

There were past lives that found you saying one thing but meaning something else. In other words, your body language didn't really match your words. You may have been smiling but anger was apparent in your eyes. This was a type of passive-aggressive behavior used to manipulate others. You were intentionally causing confusion to control people. The result was that your relationships were not based on trust or honesty but more on making sure you got what you wanted through trickery. You weren't really happy when using this technique. Your emotional states were unpredictable, which didn't make for much inner peace. Rather than having well-balanced relationships, you were left either with loneliness or partnerships that lacked a clearly defined bond.

Chameleon

In this pattern, your persona changed to meet the demands of any situation. The problems came when you grew too attached to these roles and forgot to get back to your real self. You became too many things to too many people. You usually compromised to the point of having a confused sense of identity. You glossed over your life rather than truly engaging it. Relationships lacked real depth because you were too busy acting out roles that you thought others expected of you. Your own goals got placed on the back burner. You put others first due to an overactive desire to please them.

Juggler

This pattern probably could be true of any of the three Gemini zones and was at times a nuisance for you. When you got too many plans in motion at once, it caused you great indecision. You attempted to juggle more than you could handle. This left you and those close to you frustrated. You easily lost your focus, making it hard to finish what you started. Your nervous energy multiplied the longer you procrastinated due to indecision. You loved change to the extreme and found stability boring. Commitments were broken because they infringed too much on your freedom. You were perceived as unreliable if this pattern got the best of you on a regular basis.

Interpreter

You have a long past-life history of being quick with concepts. Words entered your mind faster than the speed of light—and that's pretty fast! When you grew too impatient with the ideas of others, you were in the habit of trying to tell them how to think. This caused tension in your business, family, and romantic relationships. You were not a good listener when this pattern became too dominant. You displayed an aloofness and defensiveness that angered others. You liked to hear only what you wanted to hear, which caused you to act this way.

Illumination for the Current Life

If the past-life patterns of the Gemini Second Zone have surfaced in your present life, there are ways to heal their wounds. You will need to develop fresh perceptions to see your way through them. It will take some study, reflection, and patience to rise above these past-life influences.

You can turn Double Messages on its heels if you talk more honestly. Straightforward dialogue is the answer to a past-life habit of hiding your true intentions. Rather than putting so much energy into masking the truth, you do better when being a facilitator of clarity. You are blessed with a powerful intellect that can seek fairness, as there is a coloring of Libra ruling your Gemini zone. Strive to create harmony rather than friction. Be an advocate for unity rather than purposely misleading others. You will be pleased with the love and peace in your life. There can be a single message of happiness as you watch people wanting to work with you rather than against you.

The Chameleon pattern can be converted into a more pleasant expression for you and those around you. It gets tiring being someone you are not. Downright exhausting! Wearing an authentic role releases your creative passion. You can pass through more doors of opportunity when you walk your own talk. Rather than disappearing into a make-believe self, keep adorning yourself with innovative ideas that reflect a genuine you. Your relationships will be deeper and more meaningful. Your identity will blossom in truly wonderful ways. You will attract the luck you desire. Your own goals can come to fruition through embracing a clear sense of your identity.

With the Juggler pattern you need to gain more focus. It's not necessary to do everything at once. Learn how to compartmentalize, or at least juggle a little less. You will be less inhibited from finishing what you set out to do. People will also be less annoyed with your unpredictable ways. Don't fear commitments. Following through on them actually brings you deeper creative strength. You can find partners and friends who really care about you when you take the time to concentrate on them. You will tend to procrastinate less if you aren't pulled in so many different directions, and it will be easier to make choices. You can be free and still act responsibly at the same time.

How to deal with the Interpreter? Listen when people speak. Really hear them. Don't try to change what they say. Find some common ground. Slow down your emotional responses, and think before you react. Hold your tongue for as long as it takes to process what you are being told before you interact. You will win over more friends. Don't use aloofness as a defense mechanism—you really don't need it. You are much too smart to resort to this type of action. You have at your disposal wonderful words and concepts to negotiate fairly in this socially refined sign zone. When you play fair, you will have meaningful relationships of all types!

RoadMap to Your Empowerment

The Second Zone of Gemini is a wide highway on which to encounter diversified types of people and experiences. It encourages a vast exchange of ideas. *The key to your personal empowerment is making sure you stay true to your own self-image and pay attention to the needs of those you love.* Balancing your own identity with what others expect is a constant tightrope act for you, but it need not be tension-provoking.

You have a strong intellect. Let it guide you to make choices that deepen your perceptions and to keep being a student of life. When you take time to digest information, you give yourself time to accurately process experiences. Remember to be a good listener. There is an intense desire to impress others with your know-how. Try to create equality in your partnerships to ensure harmony. Give as much support as you receive.

Talk truthfully and people are apt to return the favor. When you are honest with yourself, you naturally are this way with others. You have a wealth of social instincts to utilize by being born in this mentally alert zone. Communication and social ease are your allies in this lifetime. Have fun exploring the many creative ways you can discover a deeper dimension of yourself.

Third Zone of Gemini: **6/11–6/21**
Third Zone Sign Ruler: **Aquarius**
Element: **Air**
Third Zone Energy Field: **Fixed**
Third Zone Signs: **Gemini plus Aquarius =**
Quick Insights about the Future

Current Life Scan for the Gemini Third Zone

Your soul was anxious to get right into life to express an inventive streak that is a lifelong gift. Being born in the Gemini Third Zone colors you with an independent spirit. Freedom is your coat of arms. You enjoy spontaneity and don't mind taking chances to reinvent yourself. You have been blessed with a sharp intellect. You prefer to make changes that are based on your own terms, as this is a Fixed zone energy field.

People can't help but notice your opinions. Your words tend to get right to the point, sometimes so much so that they send shock waves through others. You are attracted to individuals with fresh ideas, and new trends stimulate you to think creatively. You are impatient with people or groups lacking imagination. You thrive on new experiences and grow tired of routines. You like to know that your life is stable but at the same time worry about it growing too dull.

You relate well to people from all walks of like. Younger individuals enjoy your youthful vibrancy and never really perceive you as growing old. *A primary drive is to maintain a mind that never stops learning and one that inspires others to keep hoping for a better tomorrow.*

Past-Life Patterns for the Gemini Third Zone

Your past-life issues were connected to two themes. One was becoming *too aloof.* You distanced yourself from others by an extreme mental defensiveness. A second area was associated with not being able to deal with the fast mental currents running through your brain. It caused you to be *erratic and lacking focus.* You have a long past-life history of having

a powerful mind; the challenge was channeling this resource construc-
tively.

Intellectualizer

There were lives that found you relying on your mental nature in
the wrong ways. In this pattern, you were in the habit of hiding your
emotions from others. Everything was kept on an intellectual level.
You displayed an aloofness that kept others at a great distance. Rather
than expressing feelings, you put everything into a logical context. You
had the art of rationalizing down to perfection, which prevented your
lovers, family, and friends from truly getting to know you. You were "a
tough nut to crack," as the old saying goes. You could talk your way
out of just about anything with a skillful way of giving explanations.

Communication Breakdown

In this pattern, you suddenly cut off talking when a subject either
lost your interest or started to touch on feelings that scared you. You
have a great past in having a fast-moving intellect. It was typically
used to attack others if you purposely wanted to end relationships or
business dealings. This of course caused great disruptions in your life.
It was a challenge to carry on permanent or long-lasting connections
with people when you impulsively pulled away. You were self-focused
to the point of not including others in key decisions, which caused
some of these breaks in communication. When your ideas grew too far
from the mainstream or eccentric, your partnerships were damaged. A
refusal to change your thinking was yet another source of the problem.

Anxiety Prone

Your nervous system has a history of being high-strung, more so
in some incarnations than others. There were times when your nerves
got the best of you. This made it a challenge to get your goals accomplished. When you had extreme fear of the future is perhaps when you
struggled with this pattern the most. You had a lack of faith. There
were times when your internal side didn't get well-developed. You
didn't listen to your intuition that life would be okay, or you refused

to believe in a spiritual dimension of yourself. Your logical left brain kept overruling your intuitive right brain. You got lost in worrying too much about the details and lost sight of the big picture. Your health then became fragile because you were not paying enough attention to taking care of your body or mind.

Scattered Brain

When you could not stay focused, you became very scattered. You preferred to stay in control, so this was quite unpleasant for you. Actually, you had a powerful intellect that pleaded to be channeled into creative outlets, so when this energy got bottled up inside of you, it would build slowly and then suddenly erupt, going everywhere but where you wanted it to go. You couldn't get a grip. This lack of stability was frustrating for someone with so much talent. Your soul longed for peace as much as your mind did! You became frantic at times and didn't listen to advice when it came your way. You missed out on some opportunities that were right in front of you. Your mind was traveling so fast in the wrong directions that you didn't notice the doors that were open or that could be opened with some reflection.

Illumination for the Current Life

If you are experiencing problems from the past-life patterns of the Third Gemini Zone in this lifetime, you can overcome their influences. With perseverance you can channel these energies more positively. You have a very inventive mind that can develop the insights to integrate these past-life memories into clear expression.

For the Intellectualizer, you need to stop relying solely on your intellect to handle all of your life situations. You can still show off that mental acuity as much as you like! Everyone probably appreciates the way you can put complex ideas into an understandable language, but let some feelings be expressed too. Why? It gives people a more accurate barometer as to how you really feel about things. Words are great for clarifying concepts, but you need to balance them with emotions. Both worlds need to coexist. It will allow the people you want to come closer to be able to do so. Don't keep your feelings so hidden. It's okay to conceal them from those you don't want to know your secrets, but your loved ones and friends need a more accurate view. Expressing emotions is the bridge that allows others to cross over into your inner world. You will likely find your creative power may even go up a notch or two if you let your emotions be expressed. You don't need to put up an intellectual wall of defense around yourself. It's not necessary to waste so much time and energy rationalizing. If you open up, you will have a lot more energy to put into life activities and serious goals.

To get past the Communication Breakdown pattern, you need to show tolerance for the views of others. Patience is a key ingredient to keeping this pattern in its place. People will like you more if you truly listen to their opinions. There is no need to be on the attack; this only causes tension and makes compromises impossible. You need a change of strategy. It's far better to work toward harmony. You don't need to always agree to what you don't like, but you can't expect others to let you have your own way all of the time. Flexibility will be good to keep in mind. It's okay to be somewhat rebellious or to think outside the box; just be careful you don't become so unpredictable that your closest friends and lovers can't stay on the same page with you regarding major pursuits. If you can, give someone advance warning once in a while before you take that spontaneous change of direction.

The Anxiety Prone pattern can be transcended by not being so fearful of the future. It could be just too much stimuli at once that gets the best of you. It's nearly impossible to keep filtering out all of the information coming at you with your analytical left brain alone. Developing your intuitive right brain is vital to keeping you calm in the midst of a hectic world. Even in a slower one, it really helps to keep the balance between logic and intuition. It could be that you need to learn how to meditate or do yoga. Walking and swimming or other sports can help center you. A many-pronged approach to finding ways to keep down your anxiety levels is wise. Having the faith that your life will be filled with fulfilling experiences takes practice. You *can* retrain your mind to think positively. The more regularly you do positive affirmations about your life, the better it will become.

In the Scattered Brain habit, you need to learn how to stay focused on one thing at a time, which isn't easy for any Gemini. However, you can get very good at this, thanks to being born in this particular Fixed sign zone. You will get much more personal satisfaction in being able to accomplish the goals you set out to complete. You have tremendous capacity to envision a very successful future and to implement the plans to get there. But don't sit on your passion for too long, as it tends to make you mentally confused. You need to be sure to regularly take a small step toward finishing a plan. Worry less about staying in control or keeping your energies corralled; it's more important to choose strong enough structures to contain your mental intensity. Believe in your ability to follow through on serious ambitions and stay committed to your goals.

RoadMap to Your Empowerment

The Third Zone of Gemini is a land full of plentiful surprises. You can reinvent yourself when the spirit moves you easier than most can do. *The key to your personal empowerment is blending your mental and emotional natures into a rich, creative self-expression.* The more you witness your own accomplishments, the greater is your inspiration. You have a wonderful way of being able to encourage others to find the courage to realize their highest ideals.

Knowing how to tune into future trends is a gift. Use it wisely, as it could open doors of opportunity. You learned early in life that you would have to make your luck happen. Effort combined with your insights makes you a success. Finding the calm eye within the hurricane in your nervous system comes when you trust your intuition. You have a passionate enthusiasm to be happy and to radiate light into the world. Self-mastery comes when you learn those skills that best express you, and in knowing how to channel your amazing mental energy.

Cancer: The Preserver

6/22-7/21

Traditional Astrology Phrase: "I Feel"
Archetypal Theme: Securing the Self

First Zone of Cancer: **6/22–7/1**
Element: **Water**
First Zone Ruler: **Cancer**
First Zone Energy Field: **Cardinal**
First Zone Signs: **Cancer plus Cancer = Deep Longing for Roots**

Current Life Scan for the Cancer First Zone

Your soul looked forward to coming into this life to locate a comfortable niche. An early desire to establish roots or at least to find a sense of security came naturally. That's what being born in this Cancer First Zone shows. Your emotions are important to understand. This is a very watery region. Subconscious desires are ever present in you, which indicates you have to find ways to understand yourself on the deepest of levels. *A primary drive is tuning into your moods.*

You possess remarkable intuition that can be utilized creatively. Your friends, family, and lovers probably perceive you to be sensitive. They may see you as someone who reacts negatively to criticism. However, when you get the time to process your thoughts, you may be in a more forgiving mind-set.

Your moods are deep and a good barometer to how you feel. They can help you tap into your creative power when you learn how to channel their force. Business skills can be developed. You like to watch something you create blossom into maturity, as it gives you a sense of success. You can be a very caring person, enjoying plants and animals. Your home is likely your castle and you like to use it as a retreat from the world.

Past-Life Patterns for the Cancer First Zone

The past-life issues were related to two major themes. One was *clarifying your dependency needs*; there were lives when you wanted all of your time alone and then there were lives when you got too attached to others. The second area was associated with *extreme mood swings.*

You didn't always exhibit these behaviors, but when you did they threw your life out of balance.

Hermit

In this pattern, you had a tough time trusting anyone. You isolated yourself. Your emotions were difficult to express; as a matter of fact, they scared you. Feelings were foreign to your mind. Living alone worked okay when you were satisfied with having a home or pets only. It was those incarnations in which you really wanted a soul mate that the going got tough. You weren't happy living in your own world but were afraid to enter the emotional world of someone else. Fear ruled you. You had difficulty overcoming your fear of closeness. Building a fortress of defense mechanisms around you kept others away. Your sorrow was immense because you really wanted to share your life with a special someone.

Fear of Space

When you were part of this pattern, there was a dread of having time alone. You felt like you could not exist without someone always there for you. Your identity got confused because you didn't get enough solitude to figure out your own needs. When not in the presence of someone you adored, you wasted too much time worrying about when they would return. In modern terms, you were extremely codependent. Rather than having equality in your relationships, all of your time was spent pleasing others. You eventually drove someone away by obsessing over them. You were way out of touch with your emotional needs.

Moody Blues

In this pattern, your moods were too unpredictable. You didn't take enough time to reflect before reacting emotionally. Your temper got the best of you more than necessary. You exhausted yourself and people close to you when you lost control of your feelings regularly. You leaned toward getting depressed when you lost touch with the wonderful intuition that was readily available to you. Your inner voice was trying to lead you away from feeling melancholy, but you couldn't hear it. Emotional turmoil drowned out your inner clarity. You were not balancing your mind and emotions. Sometimes you lacked grounding. Your emotional outbursts got out of control, disrupting your creative flow.

Smothering

There were incarnations when you wanted to be a little too much in control of people and situations. Manipulating the outcomes didn't always make you popular. This was the part of you that didn't want to leave the results to chance. You pushed others to do what you wanted and didn't let them make enough of their own choices. Power struggles often occurred. When you could not let go of being in charge, you were met with much resistance. You would sometimes try to buy the cooperation of others. The idea was to get a certain conclusion no matter what you had to do to get this accomplished. You didn't trust very many people. It was difficult in this pattern for anyone to really get to know the real you.

Illumination for the Current Life

If these Cancer First Zone patterns are still manifesting in the current life, you can find ways to silence them or at least to get them to lessen in intensity. You will need to allow your intuition to have a stronger voice in guiding you. It will take regular practice to make peace with these past-life behaviors.

In the Hermit, you need to not be so fearful of letting someone really get to know you. It's got more to do with trusting yourself than trusting someone else. Feelings are good to experience! They can help release your creative power. Hiding from the world is shutting down opportunities for growth. You may be surprised to see there isn't anything to fear by letting down your guard. You have to take a risk in letting others into your life, just as you do in any business venture. Your mental and physical health can actually get a boost by letting someone be close to you. Solitude is good for recharging your mental and emotional batteries, but having an intimate person in your life can stimulate you to try new things.

In the Fear of Space pattern, you will be happier in finding balance in your relationships. It's exhausting and self-defeating to have a person be the sole focus of your attention. Weaning yourself away from this behavior won't occur overnight. You need to start paying attention to your own needs. Your own power needs a boost. You will need constant reminders to create goals that will empower you, and you may need to develop new relationship skills to allow you to see when you are falling back into this pattern. Finding a deeper sense of inner security is perhaps the real need here. Having faith that you can be a true equal in a partnership is a must. Time alone is good for your mind, body, and soul. Look at it as a gift rather than a problem. Learn to tune into your intuition. Don't look too much for someone else to complete your identity—you are already a whole person. Explore your creative side. Put your energy into hobbies, exercise, education, and other ventures that give you a stabilizing influence.

With the Moody Blues habit, you need to find ways to stay centered. You have a gift to tap into tremendous emotional energy, which can be poured into your creative pursuits. You need to get out of the way of this tornado-like force and channel it into productive activities. Let it work for you rather than against you. Instead of letting your emotions rule you, it's better to try to understand what they might be trying to tell you. Use your intuition. If you pause before reacting to what others say, you might be able to catch yourself before you say something you regret later. Take more time to process situations. This doesn't mean you can't act with spontaneity, just that you will find people liking you more if you don't rush into reacting before reflecting.

To rise above the Smothering impulse, you need to trust people more. You can still be a manager of your own life. Let others share in the responsibility for decisions. There is no need to manipulate. When you relinquish some control, you give good energy to yourself that can be used in other ways. You will cause less conflict when you don't constantly try to force situations to go your way. Use your competitive side wisely. It can be put to far better use in business and other endeavors.

Showing you trust those closest to you makes them want to be reliable partners. There will be less tug-of-war with those you love. Your friends will be more cooperative.

RoadMap to Your Empowerment

The First Zone of Cancer is a region for initiating action based on powerful emotions. You have an endless amount of intuition as a very valuable ally. This First Cancer Zone colors you with an innate drive to find a reliable sense of security. *The key to your personal empowerment is learning how to reign in the flood of emotions that can occur when you are in challenging life circumstances.* Finding creative outlets is vital to your happiness. Finding people who give you a sense of feeling needed inspires you. Also, establishing a home and roots that allow you to feel at peace is another important piece of the puzzle of your fulfillment.

It's true that your moods tend to run deeper than many. That's fine! Just as long as you find insightful ways to integrate this energy into creative expression. You are happiest when understanding the inner motivations for your actions. Tuning into your intuition gives you renewed faith and extra zest.

Balancing your dependency needs is a must. You have no need to cling onto someone and don't need anyone holding on to you too closely for comfort. Distance is just as essential to your well-being as is intimacy; you need to have relationships that offer both equally, or at least give you a chance to process your thoughts. You have a strong mind and an emotional nature. They play off one another, and their music is harmonious when your intellect and intuition are equal partners!

Second Zone of Cancer: **7/2–7/11**
Element: **Water**
Second Zone Sign Ruler: **Scorpio**
Second Zone Energy Field: **Fixed**
Second Zone Signs: **Cancer plus Scorpio =**
Deep Penetrating Processing

Current Life Scan for the Cancer Second Zone

Your soul knew it would have plenty of chances to experience life in mysterious ways. Being born in this Second Zone of Cancer fills you with intense emotions. These emotions are the gateway to finding your goals and friends and to expressing your passion. You came in with a longing to establish reliable relationships and emotional connections that would have a lasting presence. These partnerships and intimate life connections have to be carefully selected because you tend to form deep bonds.

Establishing a home that offers privacy and inner strength is highly valued. Your home is more than a castle—it is a sanctuary. It's not that you are hiding from the outside world; it's that you need plenty of downtime to recover from the amount of energy you pour into your work and protecting those you care about. The external world is the stage on which you act out your creative accomplishments, fight your battles, and act responsibly. Your inner world of feelings and even your residence provide your mind, body, and soul with the nourishment needed to keep you sane and centered.

A primary drive is finding a sense of rebirth when striving to leave the past behind in order to transform with a new beginning. You find it painful to let go of long-term careers, relationships, and other life endeavors. You are at your best when you learn lessons from the past, accept the reality of the present, and yet look to the future with hope and optimism. People lean on you heavily for support. It's wise to know who you can trust and who you can't. Self-mastery comes through releasing your emotional intensity into skills that release your creative power. It's important that you tune into your intuition, as that keeps you less likely to choose paths that lead to confusion. Balancing your mind and emotions comes with much practice. You gain wisdom through self-honesty. When you relinquish your worries about the past and greet the present with inspired eyes, there is no end to what you can do.

Past-Life Patterns for the Cancer Second Zone

The past-life issues for you revolved around three themes. One was *fearing your own emotions*; the internal power you possessed confused you. A second was *dependency need confusion*; when people got too close, you couldn't decide what to do with them—sometimes you grew too attached to them and at other times they became too possessive of you. A third slant was a *lack of faith*; you didn't believe enough in your ability. You didn't always act out these behaviors, but life became unbalanced when you did.

Moon Shadow

There were incarnations where your subconscious fears became too dominant. They guided you in the wrong direction, toward jealousy and manipulation. Your logic and clear reasoning took a back seat. You didn't trust very easily. Fear of losing control was usually at the root of the problem, which drove you to be extremely possessive. You were stubborn about changing your attitude. Resisting advice to adjust your behavior contributed greatly to this pattern. Unresolved anger issues kept this pattern highly fueled. You had a tendency to launch verbal attacks as a way of venting the anger. You were afraid to look within yourself for the answers; your intuition was a powerhouse, but you would not let it guide you to clarity. You lacked objectivity in not being able to accurately perceive someone else's needs. You clung to your own agenda as that felt safer, even if it meant spending your life alone.

Too Close for Comfort

This pattern found you uncomfortable when someone wanted to know you on a deep level. You tended to pull away. Why? Sometimes it was due to not being able to trust; other times it had more to do with attracting power-hungry individuals. You were bored easily with people lacking intensity, and you ended the relationship if they became too nice. The more possessive types concerned you as well, since they wanted too much from you. You had trouble defining your dependency needs clearly. Even family members and friends were kept at a distance if they started to tread too heavily on your inner world. You were extremely sensitive. It was during the lifetimes when you did not want to be a loner that you suffered the most. It was a real challenge to let someone into the world that housed the real you.

There is another interesting twist here. In some lives, you were too addicted to lovers. You wanted extreme closeness to the point of wanting all of someone's time. It still came down to unclear dependency needs. You felt insecure when you weren't with the person, and you went through too much anxiety worrying that you might lose your lover by not having more of their attention. The end result was relationships lacking fulfillment.

Digging Up the Seed

This pattern surfaced when you lacked faith in your own abilities. You didn't trust the goals you set out to accomplish, so you stopped about halfway through tasks, digging up the seed you'd just planted in order to check on its progress. The lack of completion frustrated you and those needing you to finish those tasks. This stemmed from a lack of self-esteem. Sometimes you listened to the wrong people, who talked you out of your plans. You lacked the ego strength to make good on your promises to yourself. Second-guessing your talents made you take one step forward and three steps back. Taking a creative risk was what was needed, but you looked too much for the approval of others. There were times the people you trusted purposely gave you input that threw you off of your game. Your negative thinking too often saw the future as something to fear rather than as a possibility for success.

Playing It Too Safe

The Second Zone of Cancer offers you a lot of personal power. In past lives, there were occasions when you didn't reach out enough and grab that power. You stayed too much confined in comfort zones. You gave up power to others too easily, even to the extent of trying to live out your goals through them. When you were offered new doorways to walk through, you refused to go. Reclaiming your power was not in your consciousness. Letting others take the lead was too much your mantra. You could become so dedicated to causes or people that you forgot to fulfill a few of your own goals. You hid your talent so that the world could not see it.

Illumination for the Current Life

If any of the past-life patterns of the Cancer Second Zone have resurfaced in your current incarnation, there are ways to ensure they don't continue to occur. It will take a regular effort on your part to walk in a new direction. It can be done through diligent effort!

You can cut your ties to the Moon Shadow pattern by not giving in to jealousy and manipulation. Let go. There is no need to seek to control others. If you can't trust them, do you really need them? Think of how much more time and energy you could be putting into other creative goals. You will feel like a new person when you step out of this pattern! If you have hidden anger, you need to learn to channel it wisely, as this is passionate energy that could be poured into happier pursuits. Anger turned inward eats you up and, if impulsively thrown at others, serves to alienate them. You are a very emotional person whether you admit it or not. You probably tend to keep many feelings secretive. Get better at talking them out—you are a stronger person when you do. Your mental and physical health benefit when you are honest with yourself about what you really need in your life. The Second Cancer Zone takes you into some very deep emotional water. It's important that you get to know your intuitive side, since it contains the answers to carry you to a sense of rebirth.

The Too Close for Comfort pattern can be kept in check if you define your dependency needs clearly. You need to get a better idea of what you want and—more importantly—what you need. If you desire intense people, they have to be well balanced. If you like a passionate and dramatic person, that's okay. It's good if you feel comfortable in communicating with them. Equality in your relationships is a must. If you get to know yourself on a more intimate level, you will have no need to fear anyone! Peaceful people aren't necessarily bad for you. Perhaps you need to live out your intensity in the work world or through other means. You can't be living in the fast lane all of the time. Sooner or later you will want your relationships and overall life to find stability. It's inherent in this birth zone to establish this center! Finding a sense of being at home grounds you and nurtures your success.

If you grow too attached to someone and can't face your time alone, then you are pursuing the wrong individual. You are better off with a lover you enjoy spending time with, while also having time apart so your heart can miss them. You don't want someone to be so important that you can't function without them. This Second Cancer Zone has a natural push to encourage you to find a true partner, but don't forget to protect your privacy. You lose your clarity when you have no sacred space carved out of time just for you.

Faith is the key to stop Digging Up the Seed. There is no need to start digging up your seeds when you have faith in what you are planting. Trust yourself more. Don't be so fast to look in the rear view mirror. You have plenty of time later to edit what you do, but if you keep checking compulsively on your progress, you aren't going to get anywhere. You were born with a powerful intuitive trait that can guide you through, around, and over obstacles. Don't fear the conflict; let it empower you. You won't experience growth if you don't finish what you start. Life is a process. Let what you start go through its beginning, middle, and end. Don't let negative people talk you out of your ambition and don't let them fill you with doubt. Fill your mind with positive affirmations.

You can circumvent the Playing It Too Safe pattern by taking small steps toward a new goal. It's good to challenge yourself to think outside the box, to stimulate your mind and recharge your push forward to a new horizon. You don't have to set out to change your entire world. Go slowly. Think positively. Have hope. Don't always be a follower. Initiate new experiences. Don't be afraid of showing your ability to others. You will find a renewed purpose and great vitality when you have the faith to pursue your goals. Don't fear failure—nobody wins all of the time. It's in trying to do something different that your consciousness gets stimulated with new insights. Allow yourself to be transformed by warming up to writing a new script for yourself. It's in directing your mind toward a brighter tomorrow that opportunities can come your way.

RoadMap to Your Empowerment

The Second Zone of Cancer is a territory lined with rich intuitive and emotional energy. Being born in this zone means you have strong feelings to preserve whatever you value. You can be extremely loyal to those you love, inspiring them to never stop trying to grow. Your own capacity to be relentless in making a dream come true is a gift embedded in the very fabric of this zone.

When you understand your inner landscape, you realize your entire life will be spent tapping into endless feelings. When you balance your dependency needs, life is more fun. You attract better lovers and friends when you are comfortable with your own power. *The key to your personal empowerment is in letting your intuition speak loudly through you and not fearing your talents becoming more visible.*

Communicating directly rather than keeping your thoughts hidden makes you easier to understand. Discriminating between which people you can trust and which you can't comes with experience. Realizing you don't need a person to make you whole sets you free. You have a passionate spirit that longs for a soul mate. The right person is one who respects your power but who is not afraid to confront you when you need it. You like people who give as much as they receive. When you depend more on your innermost longing to find harmony and peace, your dependency needs stay naturally balanced.

Third Zone of Cancer: **7/12–7/21**
Element: **Water**
Third Zone Ruler: **Pisces**
Third Zone Energy Field: **Mutable**
Third Zone Signs: **Cancer plus Pisces = Fueled by Causes**

Current Life Scan for the Cancer Third Zone

Your soul looked forward to coming into this life to pursue ideals and to find a meaningful sense of belonging. What indicates this? You were born in this Third Zone of Cancer, colored with the idealistic zone ruler of Pisces. You are supersensitive and don't necessarily like to reveal this to just anyone. Your intuition is even stronger than the other two Cancer zones. You are a healer, mystic, spiritualist, caretaker, and accomplished professional all rolled into one package! There is a complexity in your psyche that makes life's mysteries and symbols exhilarating to figure out. Even if you settle for traditional routes, there will be people you meet along your life journey who will direct you to explore deeper dimensions of your mind. Your spiritual quest is a lifelong pursuit. An innate search for a soul mate starts early in life. *A primary drive is to find life paths that keep you creative and hungry for learning.*

You are attracted to individuals with strong belief systems that agree with your own. You don't trust people who lack values or integrity. Your passion to put your best effort into your work is noticed by others. Caring for pets, plants, and children is a natural instinct. Establishing your boundaries to make sure you get your own needs met is a challenge—the sooner you do this, the better.

When you are emotionally confused, your patience is tested. You feel an urgency to get centered again and are grateful to people who help you stay grounded. Your creative passion is immense. You like to begin new projects, as this lifts your spirits. You tend to finish what you set out to accomplish if it keeps you inspired for the duration.

Past-Life Patterns for the Cancer Third Zone

The past-life issues for you were associated with three themes. One was *denial*, which led you astray in more than one incarnation. Another area was *escapism*. A third was *dependency need confusion*; you could not make up your mind whether to stay close or go a great distance from people. It's typical of Cancer Third Zone past-life patterns to involve a bit of closeness-versus-distance issues.

Escape to Nowhere

This pattern had its source in a fear of conflict and was saturated with running away from facing reality. You missed out on creative opportunities by not believing in yourself. You kept uprooting yourself, whether it was by moving to new locations or leaving relationships. There was a tendency to fear commitment. You had a habit of wanting to run to wherever the grass might be greener, as the saying goes. You were super idealistic but had trouble seeing things through to their completion. You liked the idea of love but became frustrated and scared by the demands of everyday life. You were disappointed by your own inability to establish roots and to find a true sense of connectedness.

Walking on the Moon

You had a problem getting emotionally confused and not knowing just how far down the road you were with this. It's true you have a long past-life history of possessing a rich intuitive side. You had deep emotions as well, and these sometimes distorted your mental perceptions. You may as well have been on the Moon for all those around you knew. You lost your sense of direction. Life went in circles and nothing got done. Procrastination became the message of the day. This caused tension in your business and romantic relationships. Your moods were like a tidal wave at times, and it was the unpredictability this pattern caused that made for a life of chaos. You had a powerful subconscious mind that sometimes flooded you with too much emotion. Your resistance to getting centered added to the dilemma.

Hide and Seek

In this pattern you were like a yo-yo. You pulled someone close and then pushed them far away with no warning. You liked to be found and then again you liked to hide. There was an extreme drive to keep secrets. Your inner world was not easy for others to get to know. You had a tendency to be more at home with a collective cause or group effort than relating one-on-one with a person. This was okay if you chose to live alone, but pain entered when you truly hungered for a soul mate but could not surrender your need for privacy. People became puzzled by your wonderful way of inviting them into your world, then suddenly locking them out. You had trouble balancing a strong independent streak with intimacy.

Clinging Close

This is yet another side of the dependency coin. There were lives where you had trouble wanting your freedom. You felt you could not live without a significant other and grew so attached that you neglected your own needs. You were a wonderful nurturing type but did not care enough for your own goals and desires. The result was not realizing your full potential. Your own creative power never really got cooking there on the back burner. Putting everyone else first left you deprived of greater fulfillment. You attracted individuals ready and willing to let you make them always be number one, and they gave little back in return.

Illumination for the Current Life

If these Cancer Third Zone patterns are still alive and well in your current life, there are ways to convert them into more harmonious expression. You will need to adjust your thinking. If any of these are long-time behaviors in past lives or in this incarnation, it will take extra effort to reverse their influences.

The Escape to Nowhere tendency can be converted into a more conducive energy for success by not being afraid of failure. It's okay if something goes wrong. It can be fixed. You can even learn from rejection or from things that need more work to improve. When you face responsibility and commitments, your intuitive side gets stronger. You need reality-testing. It's good for your mind and spirit. You will enjoy having a lover during seasons of plenty and during the leaner times. Continuity gives you a sense of belonging, which is a deep need in those born in this sign zone. Your creative power intensifies in a good way when you have support systems in place to sustain your efforts. You need reliable structures to guide your watery idealism toward clear-cut goals.

Walking on the Moon isn't so difficult to make peace with. You have one of the richest veins of intuition in the zodiac! This means you were blessed with a wonderful instinct to tune into creativity, spirituality, wealth, and love. So tap into it! You may need to get more grounded, and focusing on what inspires you is a good place to start. You should learn how to meditate, or at least sit quietly to recharge your batteries. Staying away from people or things that disorient you would not be so bad either. You need to put experiences in your life that allow you to stay mentally and emotionally balanced. Exercise, a better diet, and getting enough sleep may be needed to keep you on the straight and wise path. Being born in this sign zone gives you easy access to subconscious energies, which need to be regulated consciously. You need productive outlets for your feelings. If you are too quiet a person, it might be good to talk things out more. The solution to this pattern is closer than you might realize. You need to think positive.

In the Hide and Seek habit, you need to get more comfortable with closeness. You can still have your freedom. Trust may not come easily for you, but with some practice you can have the best of both worlds. You likely require a partner who understands your need for space. Letting someone know more of your inner world may grow easier with time. You need to be good at defining your boundaries clearly. Honest communication goes far in taking the mystery and confusion out of your needs. You need more downtime than many, and that's okay. Being born in this sign zone indicates that you soak up a lot of energy from others. This can occur in your work, friendships, or family situations. Learning how to regroup your energy makes you that much stronger in being able to enjoy intimacy.

For Clinging Close, you need to start paying attention to what you need. There is a natural devotional flow that occurs in this zone because Pisces is the zone ruler. It's important not to become so devoted to a person or a cause that you lose sight of your own identity. Severing ties with certain people, or at least getting regular time-outs, may be needed to get you back on track. It's nice to fall in love with a person or a goal—just make sure you use reality-testing to stay clear about your own objectives. You may need to reclaim your power if you have sacrificed too much of it.

RoadMap to Your Empowerment

The Third Zone of Cancer is a terrain full of inspiring possibilities. It contains endless ways to fill your plate with new ideals and exhilarating goals. You have intuition at your fingertips that others can only dream about. Let it guide you to have the faith to meet new challenges with self-confidence. *The key to your personal empowerment is learning that the past can't hold you back and the future is asking you to believe in it.*

You are happier when you have a true soul mate. You like having at least one cause to call your very own. There is a desire to know your intuition on an intimate level. It's when you are in the middle of a crisis or big change in your life that you might tap into a deeper part of your inner world. Trusting your instincts comes through trial and error. You have a powerful belief system when you achieve self-mastery.

Your creative talent blossoms when you are feeling grounded, as do your work skills. The emotions you have are a barometer to how happy you feel. Don't be afraid to talk truthfully to others. Relaxing into commitments is how you realize the inner strength you possess. When you don't hold onto a person or goal too compulsively, you feel freer. When you meet life head-on, you discover how to capture the highest truths.

Leo: The Leader

7/22-8/21

Traditional Astrology Phrase: "I Create"
Archetypal Theme: Self-Expressive Creativity

First Zone of Leo: **7/22–7/31**
Element: **Fire**
First Zone Sign Ruler: **Leo**
First Zone Energy Field: **Fixed**
First Zone Signs: **Leo plus Leo = Dynamic Self-Expression**

Current Life Scan for the Leo First Zone

Your soul was ready and raring to get here to display a bold creative passion! Being born in the First Zone of Leo throws you into the limelight maybe more than you sometimes desire. You attract attention with a fiery personality. Even when you are feeling low on energy, you can appear to be ready to blaze a new trail.

You don't make a good follower but can be quite dedicated to those willing to cheer on your most serious goals. Patience is not one of your virtues. But then again, your confidence in those you love can be awesome. You don't like to be ignored. You have a strong drive to be successful in whatever you decide to master.

Changing directions or altering a plan does not come easily. You can be accused of being too attached to your own way of doing things. People either love or detest your stubborn determination. You tend to resist change that is forced upon you. *A primary drive is to seek greater self-discovery through creative accomplishments.*

Past-Life Patterns for the Leo First Zone

The past-life issues for you were associated with three key areas. One was *excessive pride*; too much had to be centered on your needs only. Another theme was *overpowering others*; you imposed your will on others. A third area was *not usurping enough power*. This is not saying you always utilized these behaviors, only that you were off-center when conducting yourself in these ways.

Pleading the Fifth

When you did not want to cooperate with others, you completely shut down the communication. The silent treatment was one way you sent a message that you were not about to compromise. It was your stubborn resistance to change that turned people off. You tried to manipulate people by not letting them know your real thoughts. Your pride was at times so great that you hid all vulnerability, which made it virtually impossible for others to reach out to you when you truly could have used some help. Your business and love relationships didn't run smoothly because you caused people not to trust you. The Fixed energy of this zone has been with you over several lifetimes. You would not budge when your mind was set in stone.

Rule by Divine Right

In this pattern, you didn't feel any need to worry about the rights or needs of others. You were extremely self-centered. You tried to make sure you had most or all of the control in relationships, and you had trouble letting others make their own decisions. You became angry if your power was questioned. It was not easy to live with you because you were demanding of a lot of attention. Receiving was more on your mind than was giving. You lost out on people wanting to get close to you. There were past lives in which you became quite lonely after alienating your family and friends by not acknowledging their own goals.

Exhibitionist

You were addicted to attention in this pattern. If you were not hearing the applause, you felt insecure. This interfered with your accomplishments in that it caused you to freeze when fearing others were not giving you enough accolades. You lacked a strong inner world because you were too focused on the outer one. You had an ulterior motive for all of your actions, which didn't make for much peace in your life. You were constantly feeling inadequate because it was impossible for others to always be noticing you. Your mental clarity was fogged and your physical health was weakened by this drive to always be on stage.

Bruised Ego

You had a sensitive ego. It didn't take much criticism in some incarnations to get you upset. This did cause you to give up too easily on certain goals or projects that could have been successful. You needed to be more thick-skinned to keep pursuing your dreams. Your temper flared more than necessary because you let your emotions get the best of you. In some lives, you failed to claim enough power to push through opposition to your plans. There were past lives that found you so lacking in self-confidence that even a small negative remark rubbed you the wrong way.

Illumination for the Current Life

If these Leo First Zone patterns have resurfaced in this life, there are ways to make them more positive expressions. Your sign can certainly bounce back from adversity with a ferocious spirit. It might take some persistent effort to get a pattern to cooperate if it has been with you over several incarnations.

Pleading the Fifth can be overcome by not keeping your agenda hidden. You will find that open dialogue makes people want to work with you rather than against you. It will be easier for others to trust you if they perceive you as trying to be on the same team. Use that wonderful charisma in a spirit of cooperation—it is a catalyst to bring harmony into your life. There is no need to manipulate when you have so much creative energy at your disposal. Win-win situations result when you put all your cards on the table. When you need help, it is better not to let your pride get in the way, as it only prolongs your problems. Your relationships deepen when you become less afraid to express feelings. Your energy levels may even get a lift when you are not holding back so much of your true self. Loosen up and be more willing to change attitudes that are in the way of your happiness. The Fixed zone energy field is a focusing agent that serves you better when you let it flow through you generously.

The Rule by Divine Right trait requires you to be more tolerant of others. Treat people as equals and you will enjoy them that much more. The freer they are to express themselves, the more they have to share with you. Give as much as you receive. It is how your partnerships can blossom. If you are hiding behind a bossy outer show of power, it is better to come up with a new plan. You will bring people closer to you if you stop trying to control them.

With the Exhibitionist pattern, you need to have more faith in yourself. When you stop compulsively seeking attention, you start to fulfill your identity on a deeper level. You don't need anyone to complete your life but more so to share it. You need *internal* applause, meaning you need to pay attention to your inner motivations. Stay focused on developing your skills. Self-mastery of your emotions will guide you out of this pattern. You will have the freedom you really desire when you break free from this past-life hold on you. It is great to show the world your talent, and it is a natural drive for a First Zone Leo person to impress others. People will recognize you; just be your real self. There is no need to pretend to be someone you are not in order to attract attention.

The Bruised Ego pattern can be circumvented by not buying so easily into critics' opinions of you. If you have enough self-confidence, you can see your goals through to the end. Even if you experience rejection, don't let it ruin your day, week, or month. Feedback is there to let you know where you may need to revise your plan. Beware of people purposely trying to negate your projects or ideas—you may need to stay clear of those individuals. It's possible you may need to toughen up a bit. Don't let yourself be talked too easily out of your ambition.

If you are craving success too much, you need to beware of getting angry when your goals run into a setback. You are wise not to blame others. You must exercise patience, even though First Zone Leos don't necessarily find this easy. Take your time. Stay focused and ready. Another option could be right in front of you. Nobody can win all of the time. Remember to enjoy the creative process. Sooner or later you will find just the right path for you.

RoadMap to Your Empowerment

The First Zone of Leo is an enterprising terrain for all varieties of creative expression. Sometimes you may even feel like the world is your oyster, or at least a vast stage on which to act out dramatic roles. *The key to your personal empowerment is learning how to use power wisely and showing the world your ability without fear.* Being born in such a high-powered Leo zone gives you plenty of momentum to realize your dreams. You like to be admired. When you pay attention to those needing your support, you have a very meaningful life. It's important that your partnerships are based on equality.

When you communicate your weaknesses as well as your strengths, people tend to come closer. You have a lot of pride and that's probably no surprise to you. Your courage instills confidence in others. Self-mastery comes through developing your skills and learning how to channel your emotions. You can roar like a lion when you want love and attention. It's when you have the insight to notice the impact of your actions on others that your power expands in magical ways. Rather than leading by brute force, you then perceive how to lead by being a motivating force.

There isn't anything you can't accomplish. You have amazing focusing power. Be sure to change directions when you aren't getting the desired result. Flexibility is the lubricant that keeps you healthy and happy. You attract good luck when you keep a sense of humor and don't fret about the past. The future will always be your ally when you are generous with your love and possessions.

Second Zone of Leo: **8/1–8/10**
Second Zone Sign Ruler: **Sagittarius**
Element: **Fire**
Second Zone Energy Field: **Mutable**
Second Zone Signs: **Leo plus Sagittarius =**
A Playful and Highly Energized Spirit

Current Life Scan for the Leo Second Zone

Your soul leapt with joy when coming into this life. It was a chance to explore creativity and risks from every possible vantage point. Being born in this Second Zone of Leo launches you into an adventurous perspective. You prefer to act on an idea and think later. With practice you determine just how far to push your luck. You are a high-energy person. Your friends and lovers may ask you to slow down at times to give them a chance to catch up with you.

Marketing your skills or those of someone else comes naturally. You may need to tone down the exaggeration of your abilities once in a while. Your self-confidence can be a blessing or a curse. You aren't one to wait for good things to happen; seizing opportunities is more likely your approach. Learning patience deepens your skill level and adds harmony to your relationships. You get an adrenaline rush when feeling passionate about going in new directions.

A primary drive is expanding your options, because you don't like being limited in terms of what can be accomplished. This is a Mutable energy zone with Sagittarius as the sign ruler. This indicates you have an eclectic mind that wants to take ideas from more than one source. You are not as happy or creatively successful if you get too attached to one way of doing things. Learning lessons from the past keeps you from repeating mistakes. You always have one eye on the future, even when the other is fully focused on the present.

Past-Life Patterns for the Leo Second Zone

Your past-life issues were connected to two major themes. One was a false outer show of confidence caused by *denial.* Denial sometimes caused you to lack responsibility. Another was *extreme risk-taking* in which you lacked solid reasoning. This is not saying you were always acting out these behaviors, but your life lacked balance and fulfillment when you did.

Unhappy Clown

In some past incarnations, you hid your insecurity behind a smiling persona to mask your fears. This became a problem when you would not let the people closest to you be of help. Stuffing away your worries weighed on your mind. There were times you became very irritable and angry more than necessary and vented at the wrong people. You were difficult to understand because your inner world was a real mystery. You were not in touch with your emotions and this did cause great tension in your personal relations. Your creative power took a dip at times because you lost energy by not freely expressing yourself. You were blocked up! Refusing to show weaknesses took away from your strengths.

Staying Young Forever

There were lives in which you never wanted to take responsibility for your actions. Others had to pick up the pieces. You liked to get projects started but did not like to be there for the finish. Commitments scared you. A tendency was to escape from work or relationships rather than work through the problems. Conflict was perceived to be not worth the trouble. You had a youthful outlook on life and wanted to be free to dance merrily along with little confinement. People soon saw they could not count on you for the long haul. This caused you to miss out on fulfilling life experiences.

Head in the Sand

In this pattern, you lost your sense of direction. You did not want to know what your problems really were. Your assertiveness was stuck in reverse, and you lacked momentum to get your goals accomplished. There was some denial at work in this pattern. You preferred not to listen to the troubles of others, which didn't endear you to them. You felt that staying unaware of the world around you was in your best interest. The fire in you had been snuffed out. An unwillingness to adopt new strategies was the biggest thorn in your side.

Compulsive Gambling

You had no sense of limits. There was an impulsive urge to bet the farm in search of hitting it rich. You lost a lot more than you won because you kept upping the ante. You lacked enough grounded logic to know when to call it quits. The word *moderation* was not in your vocabulary. You made promises you did not keep. You meant well but lacked the willpower to follow through on good intentions. You disappointed people by not being there for them when they needed you the most. Your life lacked stability because you liked the fast lane to the extreme.

Illumination for the Current Life

If these Leo Second Zone patterns are manifesting in your current life, there are ways to overcome their influences. You have the mental fortitude to turn these challenging behaviors into productive expressions. It will take hard work but, with regular effort, you can be successful.

As the Unhappy Clown, you need to stop hiding your fears and anxieties. You don't want to keep putting up a false front; it only confuses the people you are trying to bring closer to you. Your creativity and mental energy intensifies in a more positive direction when you let your guard down. You probably don't realize how much of your energy is tied up giving out the wrong messages about how you really feel. Nobody is happy all of the time. Letting others hear how you really feel is a better way to achieve harmony with them. You will be less likely to take out your frustrations on others if you express yourself more openly.

You can get beyond the Staying Young Forever pattern by accepting responsibility for your actions. This gets easier with practice. You will like the results of turning this behavior into a positive expression: your relationships will deepen in meaning, people will trust you more, your goals will come to fruition, you will take more pride in your work, and you will get greater recognition for your accomplishments. This newfound stability might allow you to have a greater feeling of establishing roots. Facing conflict makes you a stronger person and your self-esteem rises, which is quite a payoff!

You have too much Fire in this zone to be sticking your Head in the Sand. If your assertiveness is not lit, you probably need to be thinking more positive. Your entire life will change if you stop hiding your talents. Take a better look at the world around you—there are opportunities in front of you but you have to be energized enough to find them. If you take the time to really listen to the concerns of your friends, lovers, and family members, they will want to help motivate you. You can have a mutually beneficial relationship with these people. When you run from life, you only compound your problems. It's better to keep your mind sharp and alert so you can take advantage of new life directions. You can attract good fortune by taking a positive attitude.

The Compulsive Gambling pattern requires you to see that life doesn't have to be an all-or-nothing proposition. You will need a reality-check from time to time to make sure you are being reasonable with your expectations. Taking risks is a natural expression of your zone, and there is nothing wrong with that. It's your speculative instinct that helps you tap into new trends and good business ideas. However, you need to know your limits. Balance is the key to your success. You need to be aware of when you are getting too near the edge of a cliff. Your professional and romantic lives benefit when you act with greater insight. Don't forget to notice what your loved ones need to be happy. When you keep the big picture in sight, you have a lesser chance of getting lost in this pattern.

RoadMap to Your Empowerment

The Second Zone of Leo is a large, exciting land to travel. It offers an endless number of ways to seek growth. It encourages you to keep a sense of humor as you explore means to further your potential. There is an endless inspirational wind blowing through your psyche, which can lift your spirits even when you are feeling down. There are positive currents running through the entire fabric of this zone. If you reflect enough, it isn't very difficult to see that the cup is at least half full.

The key to your personal empowerment is keeping your mind stimulated by new growth. You thrive on new challenges. Just make sure you know your limits. You will always be a risk-taker to a certain degree—it's in your mental framework to take chances. You like to lead by example. People will reward your effort when you operate from integrity. You appreciate individuals who practice what they preach. You will always feel empowered when you are true to your values. When you don't hide from conflict, your inner world gets stronger.

Third Zone of Leo: **8/11–8/21**
Third Zone Sign Ruler: **Aries**
Element: **Fire**
Third Zone Energy Field: **Cardinal**
Third Zone Signs: **Leo plus Aries = Bigger than Life Energy**

Current Life Scan for the Leo Third Zone

Your soul was pulled into this life by a strong drive to display its creative force in several different ways. Being born in this Leo Third Zone shows you to have more than enough self-motivation to accomplish whatever you set out to do. You enjoy impressing others with your abilities. You are at your best when you don't lose sight of the people who are your key supporters. You make a natural cheerleader and can pump confidence into those needing your faith.

A primary drive is having enough outlets for your fiery energy. Spontaneous impulses are a way of life for you. Being patient comes with practice. This is a Cardinal zone, meaning you have initiating sparks that propel you into new directions without much notice. Waiting for permission to do your own thing isn't really in your nature, but you make others happy when you give them advance notice before you embark on a new adventure. You can show a remarkable loyalty to your friends and lovers, which wins them over even if you do rub them the wrong way with impulsive actions.

You attract leadership roles even when you don't want them. Your work ethic tends to be strong. Having plenty on your plate keeps you focused. Channeling your inner restlessness is a lifelong challenge. You have a competitive spirit and like to dare yourself to take on a risky opportunity. When you learn your limits and how to pace your energy, you are that much more successful in fulfilling your goals.

Past-Life Patterns for the Leo Third Zone

Your past-life issues centered on three main themes. One was *misuse of anger*; venting your frustration in the wrong way got you into trouble. Another was being *too aggressive* in getting what you wanted. A third was when you *were not assertive enough*. This isn't saying you constantly got lost in these behaviors, but your life was thrown out of balance when you did.

Angry at the World

When you were not clear in expressing your anger, you took it out on convenient targets, sometimes just on whoever happened to be in your immediate vicinity. Needless to say, this was a turnoff in the human relations department. But you were really mad at *yourself*! Anger turned inward eventually funnels out in unpredictable directions. The more you tried to hold back your anger, the worse it usually got. Your health wore down as much as your mind and spirit. The baggage within you grew heavy in terms of emotional confusion. Happiness was hard to experience. Blaming others for your problems made matters worse.

Holding Back Your Creative Passion

There were lives where you were lacking assertiveness. You were too unsure of yourself. A fear of failure was sometimes at the root of this pattern. Fearing the pain of rejection, you chose to keep your skills hidden. This caused you to miss chances to advance your professional life. Even your love life suffered! You did not see yourself as worthy of success. The power that wanted to manifest through you was thwarted when you denied it access. You would not let yourself take a bold creative risk. Frustration resulted from your lack of initiative.

Blind Force

In this pattern, you had too much aggressiveness. It boiled over without focus. You were not reflective enough to have a well-defined sense of direction, and you ended up spinning your wheels. You had to start over because you missed important details. Patience was not in the game plan. Forcing your ideas didn't win admiration or friendship. You lacked commitment to finishing projects. You had tornado-like energy that needed to be channeled more accurately. Losing your wealth came from not having enough foresight to be aware of the risk you were taking.

Extravaganza

This pattern found you too identified with trying to impress the world with your wealth and power. You were hiding a deep insecurity. Buying your way through life was a way of manipulating others. An outer show hid your emotional fears and when people tried to get close, you pulled away. Your persona was one of great self-assurance. It served you adequately in the business world—it was in your private and more intimate life that you were not happy. You felt lonely but lost as to how to share a more genuine side of you. You attracted romance and friendships but didn't necessarily enjoy them. It was not unusual for someone to use your wealth for their own gain. You could have had much more joy if you dropped the false show of exuding success.

Illumination for the Current Life

If these Third Zone Leo patterns are active again in the current incarnation, you can get around their influences. A behavior that has followed you from one life into another takes constant determination in order to reverse its direction. You were born into a zone with lots of courage. With the right effort, it's very possible you can successfully transform any of these patterns.

Ceasing to be Angry at the World only requires that you take responsibility for your actions. There is no need to accuse anyone of causing your troubles. Don't blame yourself either; that only compounds the problem. Anger is an emotion. The key is tuning into what is causing you to react so forcefully. You have an immense amount of energy pouring through your mind and body. Learn how to take control of it! The more you learn how to channel this forceful stuff, the happier you (and those trying to be close to you) will be. Being a better communicator is very much needed. It's hard to get a fix on feelings and emotional intensity if you don't talk about them. Even a little verbalization is better than none. It takes practice to discuss moods and feelings. Identifying what sets you off in explosive directions is another key to neutralizing this pattern.

The key to getting over Holding Back Your Creative Passion is having more faith in yourself. You won't know just how good you are at something until you take the risk of trying. There is not much to lose in taking a chance. Look at it as a learning experience: if at first you don't succeed . . . You will find life more fun if you can lighten up about trying new things. You need to convince yourself that you are worthy of success. You need to believe more in abundance. Life will reward your efforts. Your friendships, romances, and career can improve if you are not afraid to take a first step. Letting go of your fears may not happen overnight, but you can change. It has been said that a miracle is just an altered perception. Tweaking your thoughts a little can make room for greater happiness.

Blind Force need not stay an active pattern in this life. The trick is going from reckless abandonment to greater insight. Developing greater awareness of your actions is essential. You are blessed with tremendous energy in this zone. You can scratch and claw through any obstacle, so fighting your way out of trouble is always an option. You have clearer direction when you take the time to look at all of the possible courses of action before embarking on a choice. Studying first and acting later may not be your first impulse, but it is one you need to cultivate. You lose much less time, energy, and money when you think things through first. You can still move quickly, as you are accustomed to, but aggressiveness can be toned down into well-timed decisions.

The Extravaganza pattern asks you to come out from your hiding place and learn to reveal more of the true you. Your best friends and lovers won't need a big show of wealth and fame. You can still shoot for the Moon if you like, since success is a good thing—you need it for your self-worth. But you need to develop a rich inner world to match the outer one. When you portray a false sense of your identity, it takes away from your mental clarity. There is no need to manipulate people. It is far better when you communicate honestly, as it makes your friends, lovers, and family want to bond closely to you.

RoadMap to Your Empowerment

The Third Zone of Leo is a fast-paced region packing a lot of creative zest. Each breath you take offers a refreshing glimpse of the world as a place to act out your dreams. You can excel in whatever you try to master when you learn how to harness your fast impulses. There is a spontaneous streak in you that most other sign zones envy. Let it push you to take a risk that fills you with greater self-confidence. Be generous to those you love and you will never have to look far for a friend.

The key to your personal empowerment is slowing down your actions so you can perceive your options more clearly. Use your willpower wisely and for good. Be thorough in your work and people will be grateful. Your luck changes for the better when you think positively. Balance your mind and emotions so that you can attract abundance. Don't lose sight of the humor in life. Laugh deeply. Show your inner world to those you love. Why? It makes you stronger and tightens your connections to people. Make your life a celebration with those close to you. Get to know your intuition. In the end, it may turn out to be your best ally!

Virgo: The Perfectionist

8/22-9/21

Traditional Astrology Phrase: "I Analyze"
Archetypal Theme: Desire for Order

First Zone of Virgo: **8/22–8/31**
Element: **Earth**
First Zone Sign Ruler: **Virgo**
First Zone Energy Field: **Mutable**
First Zone Signs: **Virgo plus Virgo = Meticulous Performance**

Current Life Scan for the Virgo First Zone

Your soul anticipated getting into a well-organized and busy life. Being born in the First Zone of Virgo puts you right on the front lines in dealing with details. You make a good reliable worker. There isn't anything you can't organize if your heart is in the job. Business instincts are always in your mind and easily accessed at the spur of any given moment. This is a strong, service-oriented zone. You aren't afraid to roll up your sleeves to see a plan through to the end. Problem solving is part of your life resumé.

Health and diet may be subjects of interest. You are mentally sharper when you exercise and get enough rest. There is a drive to be thorough when you find a life pursuit that captures your passionate interest. You can become compulsive in trying to be too perfect. *A primary drive is to keep perfecting your skills and to show your ability confidently.*

You believe in commitments as long as they prove useful. There is an attraction to practical-minded people. When you worry less and enjoy life more, you find inner peace. You prefer that friends and lovers share your pragmatic values. Taking a risk is not your first impulse, but you can surprise yourself and others by sensing what makes a solid investment. You like to establish routines because a structured life seems more dependable. Trying new experiences is wise, as they keep you mentally challenged and stimulated.

Past-Life Patterns for the Virgo First Zone

The past-life issues for you were connected to three themes. One was being *overly critical of others*; even your own ideas were negated by self-criticism. A second area involved a *lack of imagination*; you were afraid to dream of a better life. A third front was *excessive worry*. You didn't always indulge in these trends. But when you did, life was not as enjoyable or rewarding.

Picky, Picky

You had an ability to see the flaws in others. The problem was that you used this against them too often, which disrupted the flow in your relationships. Even your work arena was affected because people resented your criticism when it lacked sensitivity. It was a compulsive repetition of pointing out individuals' mistakes that made them upset with you. You were not very good at patching wounds you caused because your tendency was to keep right on criticizing. This was a case of possessing a well above average talent to see details but lacking the insight to shut off the verbal attacks. Picking apart the ideas of others or things you did not like caused great disharmony in your relationships.

Turning this negativity on your own thoughts and plans also held you back. It kept you from accomplishing goals. Your inner dialogue didn't make room for the positive reinforcement that you were badly in need of when this pattern was too dominant.

Too Finely Sifted

In this pattern, you were trapped by your left brain. Your logical mind drowned out your intuitive side on a regular basis. You were analytical to the extreme, sifting through ideas again and again. You didn't allow for enough idealism and dreaming to come through. You were too serious and not having enough fun. Your spiritual side was not easily accessed in your right brain although it would have been a great help when you encountered self-doubt. You relied too much on the physical plane and neglected to develop your intuitive side and give it an opportunity to help you. A lack of faith in what you could not see with your eyes or hear with your ears prevented you from a deeper understanding of life's mysteries. The romantic in you was limited in that you didn't think as much of ideals as you did of grounded earthy ideas.

Nine to Five

You have a long past-life history of putting your nose to the grindstone, as the old saying goes. This means you believed in hard work. You became fixated on working to such an extent that you didn't make time for any celebration. This intensity to achieve your serious goals made for all work and no play as a repeating pattern. Mental and physical exhaustion resulted when you did not pace your schedule. You alienated people trying to get to know you on an emotional level when you were more in love with jobs than people. You tended to worship routines. This limited your options in that you too quickly ruled out growing through new experiences.

Extreme Anxiety

You were the classic worrier. Even when you had the best that life could offer, you found ways to worry. It kept you from enjoying what you had. You were a perfectionist in several incarnations. If something got out of order or interfered with your daily habits, it upset you. A compulsive focus on lack was another side of this pattern. Your mind kept waiting for something to go wrong, even during the best of times. You had trouble staying centered. This behavior drained your energy and kept you from concentrating on goals.

Illumination for the Current Life

If these Virgo First Zone patterns have reoccurred in this lifetime, try not to worry. There are ways to navigate through them. You will need to chart a new course to get better results. It can take regular effort to make a long-seated pattern work for you.

The Picky, Picky pattern needs you to aim your mental intensity into more productive directions. Positive energy has to be carefully nurtured and grown in the same way you might build a business. It takes time and extra care to ensure its success. You need to fertilize your mind with a new type of thinking. When you stop using that wonderful intellect to criticize yourself or others, you allow for new possibilities. You attract good fortune through eliminating what has not been working for you. Your relationships can improve, in that people won't want to distance themselves from your verbal onslaughts. You can retrain your mind to not react impulsively with a critical tongue.

In the Too Finely Sifted pattern, developing your intuitive right brain helps you from getting snagged by endless details. Being born in this first zone with its repeating Virgo emphasis gives you an extra edge on any other sign zone when it comes to noticing details. This talent helps you be very efficient. Balancing this left brain natural reflex with some right brain magic is a wise thing to do. Why? It gives you extrasensory insight, which takes a load off your mind. When you only operate from the left brain, it is like being stuck in first gear and not using the other resources available to you. You could read some books on tapping into intuitive energy or take a class on working with intuition.

The Nine to Five rut becomes integrated into a creative self-expression by taking that passion for work and redirecting it into play now and again. You can do it! Children need to play because it develops their mind. Both the right and left brain hemispheres find greater balance when you combine work and play. The emotional and romantic sides of you need equal playing time. Reward your hard work by taking the time to celebrate. People will want to be a bigger part of your life when you give them a chance to participate. Hobbies, vacations, and socializing round out your life. You will have greater creative drive if you get a break from work. Your intuition gains clarity and your conscious mind finds clearer perceptions when you add variety. Going beyond everyday routines gives you vitality and strengthens your immune system.

The Extreme Anxiety pattern can be tranquilized through learning to have more faith. Nobody is without some degree of worry—you just happen to have more anxiousness than others because you have an extra sharp mind for details, being a First Zone Virgo. It's the little things that can trip you up. Try to focus more on the broad perspective and not fret so much about each small step along the way. You can go back and make adjustments. When a team is losing at halftime, they don't just quit. The coach needs to come up with a change in strategy.

You need to do the same thing. Give yourself permission to let your life get somewhat out of order. This may not be easy, but it's not as difficult as you might think. Life can get messy and then ease back in place again. Think of your projects or goals as a process. Enjoy the journey of life instead of focusing only on the destination.

RoadMap to Your Empowerment

The First Zone of Virgo is get-down-to-business terrain. Being born in this zone fills your mind with an insatiable curiosity to study a subject from the inside out. You are driven to understand details. The challenge is not getting too worried by them! Learning new skills excites you. You can excel in service-oriented professions. Finding a cause to dedicate your time to may be a heartfelt quest.

The key to your personal empowerment is communicating from your heart as well as your mind. This particular sign zone gives you an intellect that can carefully guard emotions. Giving equal time to your ideas and feelings deepens your insights. You have excellent business skills and can adapt quickly to all types of work environments.

Live your life outside of well-defined routines and you will have more fun. Your creative power multiplies quickly when you take a chance and don't live every day the same. When you allow for outside interference in your regular habits, interesting surprises occur. You meet new people and find alternative doors to enter. You usually seek stability first, and that's fine—just don't forget to try new things, because they stimulate you to see with refreshed eyes.

Second Zone of Virgo: **9/1–9/10**
Element: **Earth**
Second Zone Sign Ruler: **Capricorn**
Second Zone Energy Field: **Cardinal**
Second Zone Signs: **Virgo plus Capricorn = Self-Driven**

Current Life Scan for the Virgo Second Zone

Your soul eagerly awaited its chance to get its hands on an incarnation with well-defined plans. That's shown by being born in this time management–oriented Second Zone of Virgo, ruled by Capricorn. Clocks were probably invented for your sign zone! You hate wasting time. Your mind is well-oiled with pragmatic thoughts. Ambition started early. Marketing your ideas is never too far from your thinking. You attract responsibility, maybe even more than you like. Defining your boundaries is essential to your happiness.

You prefer to form partnerships with individuals sharing your seriousness about commitments. Going it alone is the choice if you can't find people with your same drive for completion and success. When you learn to laugh at yourself, others like you more. Making time for pleasure makes you more fun to be around. You can be a no-nonsense person to the extreme. You are a member of a sign zone that could teach courses on how to get focused. *A primary drive is establishing a structured life that will sustain your creative power and let you relax into a state of happiness.*

Past-Life Patterns for the Virgo Second Zone

The past-life issues for you were linked to three major themes. One was being a *workaholic*; you have a long history of worshiping the work goddess. Secondly, you tended to *worry greatly* about what you could not control. Letting go and going with the flow did not come easily. Thirdly, there was a tendency to be *too narrow in vision*, limiting your options. This is not saying you always indulged in these behaviors but when you did, your life was less fulfilling.

Workaholics Anonymous

So it's no big secret you didn't know when to stop working! You could still have this problem. There was no end to burning that midnight oil in order to get ahead of everyone else. A competitive streak ran through your bones. The problems came when you didn't have time for the important people in your life. You forgot they existed. Lonely days resulted in some lives, because nobody wanted to wait for you to detach from your projects. Disengaging was next to impossible once you went down the ambition highway. You were often successful in these particular incarnations in terms of wealth, but lacked closeness with people. Business went well but love was an empty account.

Worry Wart

This is similar to the Extreme Anxiety pattern in the First Zone of Virgo, but the cause here is different. In zone one, the issues came about due to being snagged by the onslaught of details; your worry pattern stems more from not feeling in control of the loose ends. You detested not being able to put everything in nice, prearranged formulas. You lacked flexibility in a big way. You would have benefited from being able to trust that everything would work out for the best, but there was no way you could convince yourself of that. Developing your intuitive right brain would have helped. Your logical left brain liked to run the show. This left hemisphere was well aware of the small things, but could not handle surrendering to a higher power or just plain trusting in abundance. You became easily tired mentally and physically from not resting your psyche when you could. An unwillingness to escape into more pleasurable activities served to aggravate this pattern.

Not Seeing the Forest for the Trees

In this pattern, you lost sight of the big picture. How did that happen? Usually it occurred through getting lost in the steps along the way. You forgot where you were supposed to be going. Rather than letting a very fine intellect with plenty of know-how lead you to the finish line, you dwelled on what was going wrong. Perfectionism was woven into this pattern as well. You wanted everything to happen absolutely as planned, leaving no room for revisions. This was of course next to impossible, as nothing in life seems to really go the way we plan. You had very high expectations for excellence. This in itself wasn't a bad thing; it was the rigid mind-set that got you into trouble. Making adjustments was looked at like having a tooth pulled. Staying focused on the broader perspective would have alleviated your worries. A lack of faith in your ability to finish what you started was another side of this dilemma.

Loss of Hope

You had a tendency in some incarnations to get down if you felt like you were not living up to your own professional aspirations. Other times you felt you were failing those who believed in you. Your self-expectations could be enormous in past lives. Putting too much pressure on yourself was a major problem. Depression came if you got too down, and getting out of these lows was a real challenge. Even in this pattern, sometimes wanting to be too perfect was the trap. Giving yourself a break would have been one way out of this. Letting go of people who were willing to help you blocked your route to happiness. Cutting off the roads to peace, prosperity, and a better tomorrow left you in limiting circumstances. Your emotional well-being suffered due to being overly concerned about external success.

Illumination for the Current Life

If these Virgo Second Zone patterns are visible in this life, there are ways to make them invisible or at least less intrusive. It will take some diligent attention to redirect their influences elsewhere. Remember, if you have dealt with any of these patterns over several lifetimes, it might take extra effort to successfully transform them.

In the Workaholics Anonymous pattern, you need to have more than work on your plate. Hobbies and spending quality time with loved ones give you the diversified life you really need. It's not good to live and breathe a job. Your health is not going to be good and burnout is a possibility. You get revitalized by pursuing other interests. A break from work allows your mental energies to get recharged. You won't have to settle for a life of solitude. Having friends and lovers gives your life greater meaning. Family members will get to know more about you than how your professional life is going. You can have deeper emotional connections with others if you are willing to make the time. Choose your commitments carefully. Balancing your ambition with some human closeness might be just the right recipe for fulfillment.

The Worry Wart challenge is solved by having more faith that life will take care of you. It's your job to make the effort to pursue your goals—it isn't your responsibility to worry yourself into a nervous wreck. You may need to develop your intuitive side or find ways to tap into this relaxing little friend. You push with maximum force to try imposing your ideas on life with your logical left brain. You need some of that right brain pause! This is how to step back and reflect. Listen to your favorite music, walk out in nature, or learn how to meditate. Do whatever it takes to get that combination of left brain common sense and right brain belief in a universal flow. Take a load off of your mind and get creative in trusting that worrying is not going to make your plans go smoother.

With the Not Seeing the Forest for the Trees problem, you need to be more reasonable in your expectations. Perfection is a real challenge for Virgos. Your zone ruler Capricorn can add to the problem because it can point to being inflexible. When you combine perfection and inflexibility, you can wind up with unhappiness. Life keeps changing. You need to adjust your perceptions to meet the new circumstances. Looking through an adjustable lens allows your life to be enjoyable. It's okay to try to work as efficiently as possible. This comes standard with your birth zone. Just be sure not to get too carried away with trying to make something perfect. There is an old saying that the whole is greater than the sum of its parts. It may be good to maintain a broad outlook on the whole picture as you work toward your goals. The ultimate finish line might be more important than worrying excessively about each step along the way. You can go always back later and fine-tune the details.

The Loss of Hope pattern can be overcome through learning not to put undue pressure on yourself. You have the very sobering and pragmatic sign of Capricorn as your zone ruler. When you combine the analysis orientation of Virgo with the seriousness of Capricorn, your mind can be telling you life has left you with no options. You need to reprogram your mind with positive thoughts. If you are trying to perform at a high level to impress other people, you may need to get out from under those expectations. It's nice to make people proud of you, but if you are only doing things to please others, you will be left with an empty feeling even if you are successful. If your total focus is on accomplishments, you are setting yourself up to fail. You need to pay attention to your internal world. Keep close the people who support you emotionally. Chances are you will feel less down with these friends at your side. At least they can help you up if you take a fall. You might need to change your priorities. Balancing material success with an inner wholeness is the key to happiness in this pattern. If you have a tendency to make things too perfect, you will need to be realistic in your expectations. This is a great sign zone to face reality, get grounded, and give yourself a much needed break!

The Road to Your Empowerment

The Second Zone of Virgo is a reality-focused climate, encouraging you to walk your talk confidently. It is a dry climate that filters out emotions, making it easier to be a methodical planner. You can excel in being well-organized. *The key to your personal empowerment is having the faith to pursue your goals and allow your feelings to be expressed.* When you tap into your emotions, your creative power is stronger. You possess an intellect with a great sense of timing changes. Your drive to finish what you set out to accomplish has few sign zone rivals.

Combining work and play relaxes your mind. When you are not being a worrier, your professional life and relationships flow smoothly. Learning how not to doubt yourself and those you love is a door to happiness. It's okay to be serious in your problem-solving—that's part of your personality and normal thinking. Lighten up when remembering the big picture, as it helps you tune into the intuitive processes that make your life seem more like a great journey. Celebrate your milestones and thank those who helped you get there. Learn from the past but don't be limited by it. Devote your life to those goals you perceive as worthy of your time. Stay loyal to your true friends and lovers. Honor your agreements. But don't fear stepping away from the reach of traditions, even just for a moment, to take a peek at new adventures that lie just beyond the borders of business as usual!

Third Zone of Virgo: **9/11–9/21**
Element: **Earth**
Third Zone Sign Ruler: **Taurus**
Third Zone Energy Field: **Fixed**
Third Zone Signs: **Virgo plus Taurus = Practical Resourcefulness**

Current Life Scan for the Virgo Third Zone

Your soul came into this life determined to seek peace and stability through finding causes worthy of your dedication. Being born in the Third Zone of Virgo gives you an extra edge in perceiving marketable avenues for your talents. Paying attention to details without getting bogged down by them is important. You tend to hold onto possessions and people, especially when you value them. Your commitment to excellence wins admiration.

You have a way of making others feel at ease with your helpful insights. Your critical eye can make someone feel unsettled if it hits too close to home. Business aptitude is part of your nature. Your ideas can make people listen, especially when they will increase their wealth and sense of well-being. You don't mind being asked for help as long as it's appreciated.

Your relationships with friends, lovers, and family lean toward the long-term. You like to stay with the familiar and known. When you have the courage to venture out into new territory, it can take you to stimulating creative heights. Keeping a positive attitude ensures better mental and physical health. You have great follow-through when you decide to finish a goal. *A primary drive is seeking meaningful work and a soul mate who will stick with you through both the peaceful and the challenging seasons of life.*

Past-Life Patterns for the Virgo Third Zone

The past-life issues for you were associated with three areas. One was too much *negative thinking*; you fought against positive thoughts. A second was *settling for less*; you gave in a little too easily on your own needs. A third area was *limited long-range vision*. When you got stuck in these patterns, life felt less rewarding.

I Can't, I Can't

You needed to be telling yourself "Yes I can!" But you weren't. You talked yourself out of trying a new plan before you even got started. Negative self-talk made for missed opportunities. You had great ideas but lacked momentum to get them going. Sometimes this was due to the wrong types of people influencing you. Negatively addicted acquaintances sabotaged your plans. You were too easily talked out of your aspirations. Low self-worth contributed to this pattern and was the source of the problem in many instances. You had the ambition but not the willpower and strength of ego needed to sustain your aspirations.

Dead-End Goals

There were incarnations that found you in very confining jobs and relationships. You allowed yourself to stay in these situations far too long. You took the service theme of Virgo in the wrong direction, dedicating yourself to people and work that didn't deserve your devotion. This kept you from being happy. Your creative power got stuffed into circumstances far beneath your potential. People took advantage of your skills, not rewarding you with what you were worth. Low self-esteem was sometimes at the root of this pattern. You didn't allow your perceptions to guide you out of these dilemmas; instead you let self-doubt be in control. You actually possessed sharp insights but your assertiveness was operating at too low a level to motivate you out of these situations.

Short-Sighted Thinking

When you were afraid to think out of the box, life became so routine that it dulled your perceptions. There were times you were afraid to think ahead. You were too attached to stability. You didn't handle changes very well because you stubbornly resisted them. Even when you were in circumstances that were turning into limiting situations, you refused to look for better options. Those close to you became frustrated with your obstinate way of hanging onto what you knew, whether it was good or bad. Better opportunities presented themselves but you ignored them. You didn't like to experiment with new ideas even if they opened new doors. Far-sighted thinking was not your first impulse enough of the time.

Abused Mind and Body

You went on work marathons that exhausted you totally. When you pushed yourself way beyond reasonable limits, the result was total collapse. You were capable of outlasting the competition but paid for it with bad health. It was a rugged determination not to quit and ignoring what your body was trying to tell you that led to trouble. Material desires were the carrot at the end of the stick that would not let you stop. A compulsive desire for success sometimes occurred. A fear of failing was another trend going on here. You would not let yourself have enough rest, thinking that if you kept working you would have a better chance to succeed. Deep survival instincts were not a bad thing—it was your unwillingness to pace yourself in a race against time that was the nemesis.

Illumination for the Current Life

If these past-life patterns are occurring once again in this life, there are ways to deal with them. You will need to be persistent in moving toward resolving their influences. With the right effort you can be successful.

To overcome the I Can't, I Can't problem, you will need to adopt a positive approach. It is wise to start filling your mind with thoughts that you deserve abundance. You can quickly pull out the weed of negative thought patterns by planting new positive thoughts. You might need to take a class in self-esteem or read books about the subject. Putting your needs first can catapult you out of this pattern. Staying clear of people who negate your goals doesn't hurt either. You were born in a sign zone that shows, with the right support from others, you can graduate to a higher degree of insight. Having faith in your ability is just the fuel to ignite you out of this pattern. Listening to your intuition could be a door to seeing your way to more fertile ground.

The Dead-End Goals rut requires you to give yourself the freedom to leave situations that no longer offer you opportunities. Break free from jobs or relationships that have long since been beneficial to your well-being. This releases your creative power, enhances your mind, and boosts your immune system. You need to perceive yourself as deserving of rewards and fulfillment. You can take the hand of new opportunities when you slip out of the hold of confining people and limiting experiences. You thrive on commitments that energize you. Rather than being drained by ideas with little reward, you need life-giving paths. You will find that open-ended life directions allow for growth. Rather than surrendering to a life of limitations, you can step into a world of self-discovery. Being with someone who shares their life with you is far better than being used by those who care little for your needs.

The Short-Sighted Thinking pattern is circumvented by not fearing change. Your zone ruler is Taurus, which is a sign that likes comfort. Life can become too passive if you are always looking for the easy way out. It's true that trying something new can bring inner conflict, but this clash awakens your drive to look further ahead. Holding on to what you already know versus taking a new path is a tug-of-war in this pattern. Stimulating experiences can get your brain to look into the future with a sense of wonder. Widening your outlook can bring greater diversity into your life. This is a good thing! Having another choice or two offers options that you might have neglected to consider. Longer-range thinking need not be feared. You can be excited by new perceptions when you don't look so suspiciously on outside interference with your comfort zones.

The Abused Mind and Body pattern requires that you learn to listen to your body when it is sending a stop signal. Being a Third Zone Virgo person, you will at times have more stamina to push ahead than many other sign zones. But when you pace your energy—resting at regular intervals and taking needed breaks—you are actually more productive. You can still be as work-driven as ever. Be competitive. Take time to enjoy life. Exercise regularly. Manage the stress. Get over the fear of not being a success. You learn through experience better than many. Your skills are likely exceptional and you can make up for any lost time quickly. Believe in your abilities. The more you take care of your health, the better prepared you are to greet new opportunities as they present themselves.

RoadMap to Your Empowerment

The Third Zone of Virgo is a gentle and curious land through which to explore life. You have endless mental resources available. Your mind has a natural capacity to put learned skills instantaneously into motion. The intellectual intensity of Virgo combines nicely with the artistic talent of your zone ruler, Taurus, to translate into perceiving the world in colorful ways. People are attracted to your soothing insights. They may not be pleased with your stubborn side but can't help but they admire your allegiance to excellence.

You like peace and comfort. When you are willing to experiment with new trends, what you already know gets stimulated with exciting perceptions. Having faith in your ability opens doors of opportunity. You then see there is no time to waste on situations you have long outgrown. *The key to your personal empowerment lies halfway between accepting the stability of the present and pushing your mind to look over the walls of your comfort zones.* Peering into the future with a sense of eagerness keeps you young in heart, mind, and soul. Your self-esteem rests upon passionately living out your values. Sharing your wealth generously with those you love keeps them close. When you look at the past with few regrets, the present with gratefulness, and the future as a new friend, you are indeed very wealthy!

Libra: The Socializer

9/22-10/21

Traditional Astrology Phrase: "I Balance"
Archetypal Theme: Conceptualization of Relationships

First Zone of Libra: **9/22–10/1**
Element: **Air**
First Zone Sign Ruler: **Libra**
First Zone energy Field: **Cardinal**
First Zone Signs: **Libra plus Libra = Social Ease**

Current Life Scan for the Libra First Zone

Your soul felt a magnetic pull to come into this life and make as many personal connections as possible. Being born in the First Zone of Libra fills you with a deep desire to seek many stimulating interactions. You may feel like you never met a stranger. (This doesn't mean you always please everyone you meet.) Through trial and error you can determine your best allies.

It is likely you were interested in finding a soul mate early in this incarnation. You thrive on partnerships. There is a heartfelt need to get feedback from those you trust. Your closest lovers and friends are depended upon to mirror back to you confirmation of your ideas. The sharing of information is part of your survivor's package and acts as a lighthouse to help you find your way during emotional storms.

Making decisions is a challenge. You like to consider your options carefully. Your ability to see situations from more than one angle can create a dilemma. Choosing what appears to be the better direction can make you uneasy. You feel a sense of relief after a decision is finally made.

You can display talent in art or music. Your sense of color is above average by being born in this sign zone. Social instincts permeate your entire being. *A primary drive is finding balance between your ideals and reality.* You are a true romantic. Finding people possessing your same valuing of inner and outer beauty is a lifelong quest.

Past-Life Patterns for the Libra First Zone

The past-life issues for you were connected to three themes. One was *hiding your true identity*; you concealed yourself, causing you emotional confusion. Another area was extreme *indecision*; making up your mind was painful. The third trend was *looking for too much in others*. You did not always indulge in these behaviors but when you did, you lost your sense of direction.

Masquerade

There were incarnations where you hid your true identity behind various personas. The problem came in when you refused to show your real self to anyone. Acting out various roles became too dominant. You were out of touch with your feelings, which caused great emotional confusion. Your relationships stayed on the surface, lacking depth. You didn't trust others. Professional success was solid but your private life stayed lonely. The longing for closeness with a special person stayed out of your reach. An unwillingness to drop the masks kept people at a distance. Your identity lacked clarity because you were spending too much time extending outward, hoping to be what others expected you to be.

Sitting on the Fence

Waiting too long to make decisions proved frustrating for you and for those waiting for you to make up your mind. Procrastinating in acting on one choice over another caused you to miss out on opportunities. Nervous anxiety sometimes resulted from this painstaking proposition of choosing. You had a great ability to perceive options, and it was the emotional attachment to having too many choices that brought tension into your life. There were times you felt guilty about leaving someone out of the equation, which contributed to this pattern of indecision. Another cause of this behavior was a fear of making a choice that displeased others. Pushing away those who were trying to get you off the fence only added to this dilemma.

Please Fulfill Me

Looking for too much of your identity in others caused this pattern. You have a long history of desiring a soul mate. It was only when you lost track of your boundaries that you got into big trouble.

You weren't feeling fulfilled when you grew too dependent on others for happiness. There was sometimes a compulsive feeling that you couldn't live without a lover's constant attention. This prevented you from developing a deeper sense of your own needs. You had a strong intuitive part of you that could have guided you away from partners not good for you, but your yearning to be accepted was so intense that your intuition was not able to be of assistance. Reality-testing was missing as well.

Super Compromiser

You had a nagging itch to please people. This caused you to give in too easily in negotiating for your own goals. You had a sharp mind with great insight. Believing that you deserved more was lacking. Low self-esteem fed into this pattern. Letting yourself be talked out of a plan delayed your happiness on more than one occasion. Being more assertive was a challenge. You didn't have enough faith in your own ideas. You wanted so much to make others happy that you left yourself out. Being liked at all costs did prove expensive.

Illumination for the Current Life

If you are still confronted by these past-life patterns, you can heal their wounds. You will need to make a constant effort to deal with them. With practice and patience, you can lessen the impact of these patterns.

Overcoming the Masquerade pattern requires that you embrace your real identity, or at least make that your goal. It can be disorienting trying to be too many selves for others. You owe it to yourself to be true to your own goals. It is exhausting and very time-consuming to portray someone you are not. Your real friends like you the way you are. The authentic you is the deeper part of your identity and the key to self-discovery. You get a genuine closeness with people when you drop the acting roles. Your social instincts are powerful thanks to being born in this sign zone. Have fun with them! Be sure to lock onto the inner part of you that is the real thing. Your creative power gets stronger when you assume your inner depths.

You can stop Sitting on the Fence by putting more trust in your decision-making power. It is actually less painful to live with your choices than it is to agonize over which ones to make. Reflection is a good thing. However, if you stew too long, clarity can be lost. If you regularly delay making decisions because of guilt, you need to get better at having greater faith in yourself. The guilt is not helping you answer a question. Your inner strength increases when moving forward with a plan. Weighing options comes naturally to you as a First Zone Libra. The scales of justice rest upon the symbolism found in your sign. If you think in terms of fairness and what might lead to a win-win solution, you are on the right track to overcoming this pattern.

The Please Fulfill Me pattern requires you to stop looking for perfection in others. There are no perfect people, so nobody can really give you everything you require. First you need to see that you came into this life already complete. You don't need to look to someone else to fulfill you. Equality in your relationships is what you really need. Clearly defining your boundaries is essential to your happiness. There is no need to anxiously crave the attention of a partner. Developing your own identity is the passport out of this pattern. Getting to know yourself on a more intimate level makes the path to bonding deeper with others. When you are with a true soul mate, there is a natural balance that takes place. Your commitment is a mutual agreement made from love rather than addiction or demands. You will enjoy the freedom you will have when you break from the hold of this pattern.

To get past the Super Compromiser habit, you need to get bold in asking for what you need. Say No when you mean No! You will find your goals easier to meet when you aren't always giving away your power. Make people earn your cooperation. If you cave too quickly, your own needs become the last priority. You might need to be more of a squeaky wheel in order to get noticed. You will be less frustrated if you learn to stand your ground. Believing in your ideas comes with practice, so give yourself permission to fight for them. You will be less angry at yourself and others if you are direct in your negotiations. This could be a part of your personality that you have not used much in the past. Exercising your assertiveness gets easier with regular practice!

RoadMap to Your Empowerment

With the repeating emphasis of the sign Libra, the First Zone of Libra is fertile terrain for building successful relationships. Filling your life with people who stimulate you to think boldly and creatively is heartfelt. *The key to your personal empowerment is aligning your mental perceptions with your creative passion.* When you do this clearly, you are never very far from the road to happiness.

Keep your own goals well-defined and undiluted by what others need. The peace and stability you seek depend on being decisive. It's great to be aware of all choices possible, but it's more liberating to live with your completed decisions. You can always revise them later. You are less anxious and more spontaneous when tuning into your intuition—a key friend in helping you avoid people who don't have your best interests in mind. Being an air sign, you have a strong intellect. Lacing it with emotional strength puts you on a journey you will never regret.

Second Zone of Libra: **10/2–10/11**
Element: **Air**
Second Zone Sign Ruler: **Aquarius**
Second Zone Energy Field: **Fixed**
Second Zone Signs: **Libra plus Aquarius = Social Excitation**

Current Life Scan for the Libra Second Zone

Your soul felt great anticipation to come into this life and encounter people from all different backgrounds. You really like days that are unique, setting themselves apart from previous ones. Being born in the Second Zone of Libra spells plenty of exciting social experiences. Moving suddenly in new directions is caused by individuals and groups you meet along your journey.

Relationships can start and end abruptly until you find that right soul mate. You like individuals who aren't afraid to speak their mind, but you appreciate them more if they are sensitive to your feelings. Some may perceive you as aloof. You usually explain this as your way of acting casual. Freedom is highly valued. When someone treats you as an equal, you tend to trust them.

Your creative drive can be very spontaneous. Your mind is inventive. Being in the company of innovative people motivates you to pursue your goals. You prefer upbeat minds over the ones that play it too safe. You love peace and quiet in your home because it is where you get recharged. You don't mind taking a risk once in a while if it has a well-conceived strategy behind it. *A primary drive is maintaining a sense of direction that is aligned with your values and need for inner harmony.*

Past-Life Patterns for the Libra Second Zone

The past-life issues for you were associated with three themes. One was *extreme competitiveness* that lacked a sense of fairness. Another area was *aloofness*, which was used as a defense mechanism. A third was *surrendering your individuality and freedom.* This does not mean you always portrayed these behaviors, but when you did your life lacked clarity and happiness.

One-Upmanship

In this pattern, you believed in winning at all costs. You were not aware of what others needed, because your self-focus was immense. It was difficult to get to know you, as your mental defenses built a wall around you. This was taking competitiveness too far. You made the rules up as you went along and they had to benefit only you. Attacking the ideas of others was your first impulse. A spirit of camaraderie was missing. You tended to be a lone wolf type. Your thinking did grow eccentric in some incarnations. Goals that were very self-serving caused conflict in your relationships. You were not one to compromise. There were rebellious urges that made you difficult to count on. Unpredictable behavior that changed directions suddenly kept people on the defensive. This was sometimes how you tried to stay in control—by being hard to figure out.

Cold Shoulder

There were past lives that featured an intellect that was sharp but not very warm. You were cut off from your emotions and had a way of not showing enough empathy for the problems of others. You hid your feelings behind your intellect. You were fast with ideas but not so quick in letting anyone get close. There was closeness and distance regarding relationships. This means you let someone feel like they were going to be allowed into your inner world and then you suddenly chased them away. There was inconsistency in your romances because you feared commitments. You became very aloof when distancing yourself from a lover or friend. It was your way of staying in absolute control. You feared becoming vulnerable.

Groupitis

In some lives, you regularly overidentified with groups. This was your way of feeling secure. The problem was that you were not in touch with your own uniqueness. The group identity tended to dominate your thinking. You were really hiding from the world. You lacked faith in your own ideas. Being too much of a follower limited your opportunities. Your thinking became limited in scope. The group mentality ruled you. Your devotion was often taken advantage of by others who were more than willing to take everything you were giving. You too often didn't get back nearly as much as you gave away.

Loss of Direction

This pattern usually resulted from letting others dictate too much of your future. You lacked the ego strength to fight for your own rights. You had good ideas but no faith in them. Often there were people in your life not giving you encouragement to pursue your dreams. You had a tendency to believe in the wrong individuals, those who weren't good at offering positive energy. You let chances for new directions go by when you thought about them too long. You had a strong mind but needed some fire to get moving. You didn't feel the freedom to break through into stimulating new options.

Illumination for the Current Life

If you are still encountering these past-life patterns in the current life, there are methods to lessen their influences and even to get them to totally disappear. It will take regular practice to make sure you really get past these habits.

One-Upmanship is resolved by being a team player. This isn't saying you can't be an individualist as needed. Balancing your own needs with that of someone else is the right plan. You will have harmony and fulfillment in partnerships when you have a strategy that is mutually beneficial. With Aquarius as your zone ruler, you probably enjoy keeping one foot out of the box. This means you cherish having your own unique goals that may even go against the norm occasionally. When you support the goals of others, you win their friendship and cooperation. Rather than impulsively going on the offensive with your ideas, you further your own plans by being willing to compromise.

The Cold Shoulder pattern can be overcome by warming up to your emotions. Being less fearful lets others come closer. Relinquishing absolute control will actually feel good, as it releases your creative energy. You have a strong intellect and can become better at communicating feelings. People will trust you more when you reveal some of your inner world. When you act less aloof, your partnerships deepen in meaning. Relationships will stabilize when you don't suddenly pull away. You have a great capacity to be both a friend and a lover. When your fear isn't ruling you, it's possible to come out of the cold and establish long-term alliances.

The Groupitis tendency lessens in intensity if you stay true to your own unique identity. Groups can be a wonderful thing. They can be supportive and help us maintain a clear sense of direction. Just make sure you define your boundaries carefully so your own needs get met. The causes you value may require a group involvement. Be sure a group affiliation is worthy of your dedication and that you are getting something back. Your ideas are likely admired by groups. Your mind can be innovative and trend-setting. Make sure you get some private time to keep your own plans on track, independent of group influences. Balancing your personal ideals with those of others is a lifelong test.

In the Loss of Direction pattern, you need to act on your ideas. The Air element gives you plenty of intellectual energy. There are times you will need to have the faith to push forward. It's okay to make mistakes—you can correct them later. If you are hesitant because of negative input from others, it will be necessary to steer clear of their influence. It will not take long to find the confidence you need when in the company of supportive people. You are much too progressive in thought to hold your insights back. Your creative power is maximized when you are in motion. If you are feeling bombarded by too many options, take some quiet time to process. You can focus more easily when you take a moment to contemplate your options. You aren't one that functions well under pressure, so take a time-out and think things over—but don't forget to move forward!

RoadMap to Your Empowerment

The Second Zone of Libra is an idea-producing terrain full of rich insights. Being born in this freedom-oriented region with Aquarius as the zone ruler encourages you to desire plenty of mental latitude. You will likely travel to various longitudes in search of new experiences. You enjoy meeting people from diverse backgrounds. *The key to your personal empowerment is integrating a passion to further your own goals with recognition of your impact on others.* Communicating your feelings as well as your concepts deepens your bond with those you love.

Having faith in your goals ensures a happy future. You like to know there are options to each path you choose. Individuals who stimulate your mind have a great chance to win your heart. You like having your values and causes respected. There is a passion to fight for your ideals. You yearn to find a lover who is able to be a friend as well. Your loyalty is won by those supporting your freedom. Your creativity grows quickly when you are true to your identity. You are happiest when thinking positive and acting spontaneously on your thoughts.

Third Zone of Libra: **10/12–10/21**
Element: **Air**
Third Zone Sign Ruler: **Gemini**
Third Zone Energy Field: **Mutable**
Third Zone Signs: **Libra plus Gemini = Social Curiosity**

Current Life Scan for the Gemini Third Zone

Your soul was excited from the beginning of this incarnation to get the opportunity to pursue all types of learning. Being born in the Third Zone of Libra allows you to encounter people from diverse backgrounds. You have a strong appreciation for beauty, which can lead you to enjoy art and all types of color. Your personality radiates magnetically, attracting support for your ideas. Exchanging information with others helps you keep your goals clear.

You can excel in teaching and writing with Gemini as your zone ruler. Working with the public is a natural talent. You are curious about what makes people think the way they do. The search for a soul mate able to keep up with your fast-paced mind is a heartfelt need. You enjoy individuals with a sense of humor. You are not fond of nervous types because they make you anxious. A longing for inner peace causes you to unwind through taking time alone.

A primary drive is seeking mental stimulation through travel, books, and lively communication. Without this, you feel like a fish out of water. You detest boredom. People who refuse to change or mature in their knowledge irritate you. You perceive life through intellectual glasses but desire a soul mate with a big heart. You enjoy celebrating your milestones. Creating traditions of your own liking is a favorite pastime. Spending time with friends and lovers wanting to share their wealth of life experiences is something you treasure. You respect the past, like to keep the present beating to a lively drum, and long for a future lined with a promise of new inspiring experiences.

Past-Life Patterns for the Libra Third Zone

The past-life issues for you were connected to three areas. One was *manipulation*—using a very sharp intelligence to control others. A second was *being too dependent on others*; your own identity got confused in the process. A final trend was a *nervous insecurity*, caused by a lack of confidence. You didn't always get lost in these behaviors but when you did get hooked by them, your life was not as fulfilling.

Compulsive Strategist

You had a powerful mind that knew its way around any communication avenue. You sometimes manipulated people by purposely steering them away from what you really wanted them to know about you. Concealing your feelings behind intellectual armor made you appear very distant. Your desire was to control the outcome of situations. You preferred to have most of the power in partnerships. This caused disputes that could have been avoided through compromise. You didn't like to reveal much about your feelings. It was difficult to establish a true bond with you when you displayed this pattern. You were often successful in professional endeavors but lacked the fulfillment of an intimate personal connection. Your self-focus was your true loyalty. Power struggles ensued when you pushed your own agendas too far.

Staying in Shallow Water

If trapped in this pattern, you preferred to avoid feelings altogether. You traveled too much on intellectual highways. Life became quite dry. Why did this happen? Usually it was a fear of experiencing emotions. Shallower waters meant you didn't have to get over your head in emotional entanglements. You did have problems when individuals wanted more emotional support from you. The intellect in you could not let go. Your intuitive expression was spontaneous when it came to handling business. You could pour this energy powerfully into creative work, but when it came to love and intimacy, you shut it down. It could have guided you to be more feeling-oriented, but you couldn't go there. You did miss out on more closeness in your life because swimming out into the emotional depths with others was off-limits.

Flattery Will Get You Everywhere

There were incarnations where you were so starved for love that you could easily be fooled by kind and sweet words. People tuned into your neediness and used it to control you. Your dependency needs were out of balance. You wanted too much from someone. Your self-esteem was low, which added to the intensity of the pattern and made you more vulnerable. Denying how you felt caused you to remain in unfulfilling relationships, even when someone gave very little love back to you. Your identity became confused as you looked for too much approval from others. Being assertive for your own needs was missing.

Anxiety Ridden

Your nerves were unpredictable when this pattern was accentuated. Worrying about what you could not control was often at the root of the problem. Irrational fears surfaced when you lacked faith in your own insights. You were too easily confused by individuals with strong opinions. Your health suffered the consequences when you obsessed about situations. Your inner world was shaky because you too often relied solely on your left brain logic; if you had reached out to your intuitive right brain, you could have felt the inner tranquility you so badly needed. Even when your closest friends and family attempted to console you, your worries tended to stay in control of you. Too many of your goals went unfinished due to the impact of your anxieties.

Illumination for the Current Life

If these past-life patterns are still a concern in this lifetime, there are ways to lessen their impact. With regular practice and patience, you can transform these behaviors into more productive expressions.

Stop being a Compulsive Strategist by being open about your ideas. When you don't hide your agenda, people will see that they can trust you. Having faith in yourself and realizing it isn't necessary to be in absolute control opens the door to healing this pattern. Using your intellectual prowess to bring harmony into your partnerships is a far better tactic than manipulation. You will experience fewer power struggles if you are honest in your communication. You will have a lot more energy to put into creative accomplishments if you stop focusing so much time on misleading others. You will likely be surprised to see how much better you feel when being direct. The intimacy in your romantic encounters multiplies when you come out from behind the mask of an overly protective intellect.

The propensity to stay in Shallow Waters is reversed by giving yourself permission to be a bit more feeling-oriented. It may scare you at first to venture out into emotional territory with a person, but this could prove to deepen your identity when you see there is nothing to fear. The giving and receiving of emotional support in a relationship deepens the trust. You will sense a clearer commitment with someone when you expose a few feelings. Your creative power expands when you find the freedom to speak not only from your mental plane but from the emotional ocean within you as well. This is essentially one of the great gateways to your intuition: communicating from the feeling side of your psyche. Balancing your mind and emotions makes you a match for any pattern!

Flattery Will Get You Everywhere is met head-on by redefining your boundaries in relationships. You must know the middle—that line in the sand you can't cross—in order to maintain a clear sense of identity. Nobody can give you everything you need. What you are seeking is within you! It is wonderful to find that special someone. But first you have to fulfill your own internal needs so you can enter a partnership not being too dependent. Being assertive to ensure you are an equal is a must. Your birth zone requires that you be independent in order to have a successful relationship, for only then you can join forces with a lover. Flowery words from a person must be backed up by action. You need to know what you need from a partnership. Giving and receiving must occur equally, or you are in the wrong relationship. Denial prolongs problems. Learning to reality-check your alliances with others saves you time, money, and energy!

The Anxiety Ridden trait need not be a constant source of aggravation. You were born into a sign zone that has Gemini as the zone ruler. This fast-moving mental sign, along with your airy Libra Sun sign, points to extra nervous energy pumping through your brain synapses, which you probably endure on a daily basis. Learning how not to panic when bombarded by too many experiences at once may take practice. You can't solve all of your problems at the same time. Compartmentalizing may be part of the answer, which means you will focus on one part of a puzzle at a time. You need to feel in control of your life. Developing your right brain through meditation and other methods of relaxation can provide relief in times of stress. Learning techniques to help you better prepare for nervous episodes is wise. If there are people and situations acting as triggers for anxiety, you may have to decide if you can continue to tolerate their intrusions on your peace. More of your plans will get fulfilled if you can find ways to calm your nerves.

RoadMap to Your Empowerment

The Third Zone of Libra offers an endless world of stimulating relationships. You are the natural networking type. You can't help but enjoy people-watching. Staying abreast of the news in your community or even what occurs globally is an interest. *The key to your personal empowerment is tuning into your own identity while in the midst of deepening personal commitments to others.* You attract relationships easily. Sometimes they start faster than you expect. Staying true to your own goals is a must. Being emotionally supportive to those you love ensures greater longevity to your partnerships.

You have great communication skills. Sharing ideas can pave the way to exciting opportunities. Having faith in your goals is vital to getting them accomplished. When you are clear about your self-worth, your life naturally falls into place. You have a delicate nervous system, and taking time to rest and relax improves your immune system. Letting your intuition grow in strength points the way to inner peace. When you give equal time to your spiritual, mental, and emotional dimensions, you live life with clear eyes and the vision to fearlessly walk into the future.

Scorpio: The Transformer

10/22-11/20

Traditional Astrology Phrase: "I Empower"
Archetypal Theme: Power Instincts

First Zone of Scorpio: **10/22–10/31**
Element: **Water**
First Zone Sign Ruler: **Scorpio**
First Zone Energy Field: **Fixed**
First Zone Signs: **Scorpio plus Scorpio = Penetrating Focus**

Current Life Scan for the Scorpio First Zone

Your soul longed for a chance to explore life in an introspective and passionate way. You were born in the First Zone of Scorpio, indicating that your emotions become intense when you find subjects that capture your attention. Your life is a series of awakenings of your creative potential. You have a tendency to bond deeply with people you trust. Finding a profession that makes you feel alive and even reborn is an inner quest.

A primary drive is experiencing a clear sense of your personal power. Without it you are lost; with it there is no end to how deeply you can be fulfilled. You avoid power struggles when you are honest about your motivations. Your need for privacy has few rivals from other sign zones. When you reveal your inner world to a lover, family member, or close friend, you expect their loyalty. You detest being betrayed, and it can end your connections to people. When you learn how to forgive, you do grow immensely. It doesn't mean you need to forget, but it helps when you can let go of the past through a clear processing of it.

You can have an attraction to the mysteries of life and the meaning of symbols. To a certain degree you are a natural psychologist. Understanding the inner workings of people and things intrigues you. Figuring out problems and puzzles can be a fun challenge. There is a business savvy that can be marketed. You have the instincts to be a good negotiator.

Your life is happier when you are honest with yourself. Expressing your feelings keeps you from getting mentally confused. When you are direct in dealing with a problem, you find life more energizing than when you brood. Allowing your talent to be seen opens up new possibilities for success. When you learn to be aware of your impact on others through your actions and ideas, you attract better luck and abundance.

Past-Life Patterns for the Scorpio First Zone

The past-life issues for you were linked to three themes. One was *repressing your emotions*, which caused you to block your creative power and found you sitting too long on your anger. A second area was the *over-use or under-use of power*, this disrupted the flow in your relationships. You were either too forceful or not assertive enough. A third direction was *manipulating* situations to work out on your behalf only. When you gave into these tendencies, your life lacked balance.

Toxic Waste

You were out of touch with your feelings in this pattern. You held back your emotions, which eventually poisoned your thoughts. Your perceptions were too distorted from hiding the way you really felt about things. This got in the way of your creative expression. You did experience a lack of confidence that caused you to miss out on opportunities. Your health sometimes suffered because you were carrying around too much bad energy. If you could have talked through your feelings, you would have had a better chance to escape from the clutches of this pattern. The intuitive part of your consciousness would have been a great tool to utilize to get you through this challenge. It stayed too dormant due to hiding your emotional intensity.

Under My Thumb

There were incarnations where you were in the habit of overpowering others. You feared losing control. People were not permitted to get too close, so getting to know the real you never really happened. You were quite successful in business because you knew how to win. You didn't do enough to encourage the personal power of others because you were too busy hogging all of the attention. Your own goals were the only thing important to you. Your self-focus was very dominant. You were very insecure and used this tactic to preserve your lifestyle.

In some past lives you acted out the part of the victim in this pattern. You didn't claim your power, giving it away too easily. You lacked self-esteem. A lacked of assertion kept you in limiting relationships and jobs. You were too easily intimidated by those who seemed very confident. Your resources and time were too often abused by others. You had unclear dependency needs and lost sight of the boundaries you required to be your own person.

Chip on Your Shoulder

This was an anger you turned inward. Why? Sometimes this was due to blaming others for your shortcomings. You looked for a scapegoat to make yourself feel better. Then there were occasions you resented those who appeared more successful. You were jealous of their good luck. Your emotions were bottled up and you didn't do a good job of expressing them. You chose to stew in your own unhappiness for long time periods, which resulted in feeling very low and having bad moods. Your sense of direction got stymied because your focus was glued on the past. Rather than processing your way through life with honest assessments, you were in a state of denial. You didn't like yourself, which produced tension in your relationships.

Erupting Volcano

This was an anger you turned forcefully outward. You sat on strong feelings for far too long until they boiled over, exploding at whomever was in your path. This pattern disrupted your stability. People wanting to form close relationships with you were reluctant when they became the target of your unhappiness. You didn't do well in forgiving others. Holding grudges kept you at a distance from the very people who could have helped you the most. You were very passionate, but not able to successfully channel that powerful energy productively.

Illumination for the Current Life

If these Scorpio First Zone patterns are presenting a problem in your current life, there are ways to counteract their influences. However, it will take some persistent effort to ensure you are successful in overcoming their pull.

In the Toxic Waste pattern, you need to get better at not holding so many of your feelings inside. Feelings can be the power behind your creativity rather than a force pushing against you. Your intuition rides the waves of your emotions if you let them flow more freely. Your intuitive side runs deep and can guide you quickly out of this pattern onto the higher ground of clarity. Your health improves immensely when you express your emotional intensity. You were born into a sign zone that demands you be more direct in communicating. Hiding your feelings is swimming against your zone's powerful currents, which flow through your consciousness outward. Holding too much in confounds your thoughts. You attract good things when you courageously share more of your inner world.

The Under My Thumb pattern requires that you relinquish some control if you are overpowering people with your demands. You will actually get the best that others offer when you allow them the freedom to be themselves. Equality in your partnerships heals this pattern. You will find true love when letting someone see a bit of vulnerability. A false outer show of strength only serves to keep people away. So by supporting the goals of others, you get more of what you need. All of your relations improve when you seek fairness on the playing field. Letting go of your fears occurs by learning to trust.

If you are on the other side of the coin and not claiming adequate power, you must learn how to be assertive. Your relationships will lack balance if you give away too much power. You have to step up to the plate and demand an equal say. Your creative passion intensifies in a more satisfying way when you express your ideas openly and directly. It's okay to be sensitive, but staying passive will not lead to happiness. To reach your own goals, you have to act courageously. Even taking a small step into this brave new world will feel like you have reinvented yourself. You can be liberated from this pattern by believing in yourself. Redefining your dependency needs and boundaries is a must to fulfillment.

That Chip on Your Shoulder can be overcome by taking responsibility for your own mistakes. Taking a more positive attitude is the best medicine to heal this pattern. Staying stuck in the past due to jealousy and wishing you had someone else's life is not the answer. Creating new goals and passionately pursuing them is wise. If your expectations for yourself have been too high, it is okay to lower them; you may need to be more realistic in what you can accomplish. Anger is a raw emotion. Learning to express your feelings is a great way to start lessening the intensity of this pattern. You are blessed with creative power and you need only redirect it to find the harmony you seek.

The Erupting Volcano pattern requires you to get in touch with your moods and feelings. Instead of releasing your pent-up anger onto others, it is far better to talk things out earlier. Holding onto your anger for much shorter time intervals is wise because it won't be as intense when released. You will have more closeness and happiness with loved ones when you learn how to channel this forceful energy productively. You will be less likely to hold onto bad feelings toward others if you get better at communicating what's going on within you. The payoff for getting past this behavior is stability, increased love, and a much more abundant life.

RoadMap to Your Empowerment

The First Zone of Scorpio is a passionate climate. It has waterfalls of creative power just waiting to empower you. It takes a bit of intuition and reflection to tap into this mysterious place. *The key to your personal empowerment is acknowledging your weaknesses and having faith in your strengths.* What you resist persists; when you don't try to hide your insecurities, they have less power over you. Flowing with change rather than thinking you can control it gives your creative impulses greater success. You thrive on privacy and need to have a regular dose to keep your mind, body, and spirit in sync.

Being angry at times is fine; letting that anger rule you is not. Look to strike a happy medium between releasing your emotional intensity and understanding the consequences of those actions. Be patient in taking in the whole picture, as that will bring you stability. Seeking equality in your relationships keeps your dependency needs in check. Using your power wisely is a gateway to harmony. You experience rebirth when having the courage to reveal your inner world to those you love and in showing the outer world your talent.

Second Zone of Scorpio: **11/1–11/10**
Element: **Water**
Second Zone Sign Ruler: **Pisces**
Second Zone Energy Field: **Mutable**
Second Zone Signs: **Scorpio plus Pisces = Vivid Imagining Power**

Current Life Scan for the Scorpio Second Zone

Your soul was excited to enter this life, knowing the magical use of intuition would be readily available. Being born in the Second Zone of Scorpio frees you to imagine a life that brings you fulfillment and inspiration. The trick is taking pragmatic steps to execute a well-conceived plan. You have the gift of aesthetics and intuition readily available by having Pisces as the ruler of your zone.

You have a passion for ideals. It's vital that you are clear about which causes are worth fighting for and which are mere illusions. Sound reality-testing is an ally you must cultivate in order to avoid getting lost along your journey. You enjoy having friends from many creative paths. Your romantic impulses are stronger than the other two zones of Scorpio, and a longing for a soul mate was probably awakened in you early. Someone sharing your values is desired. You have a need to fall in love over and over again—with a lover and with your most cherished life paths. Your commitment to friends, family, and lovers tends to be stronger if you keep your expectations reasonable. There are no perfect people and it's important for you to realize this as early as possible.

A primary drive is having the faith to put into practice your highest beliefs and ideals, along with a healthy respect for reality. You enjoy inspiring others to live out their visions. Keeping an open mind allows you to perceive the future with clear eyes. You find your personal power through the love you feel and the passion you put into your creativity.

Past-Life Patterns for the Scorpio Second Zone

The past-life issues for you were connected to three themes. One was *surrendering power too easily*, causing you to lose your clear sense of self. A second was a *lack of faith*; you stopped believing in your potential. A third area was *extreme emotional disorientation*, which caused you to lose your sense of direction. This isn't saying you always engaged in these behaviors but when you did, life was not as enriching.

Waterlogged

You soaked up so much energy from people that you forgot to disengage from them. The result was emotional confusion. Your sense of boundaries was not very keen. Guilt was often the reason you overidentified with the problems of others. You were very sensitive, and criticism from others stopped you in your tracks. You had a powerful intuition but it was stuck. Your mind gave you too many negative messages about your potential. Your momentum would stall because you didn't believe enough in your ability. When you took time alone to recharge, you spent too much time worrying about what you were doing wrong. Trying too hard to please others took you off-track as well.

Idealism Lost

You had a strong vision about what you wanted from life but often lacked the reality-testing to get the desired results. Perfectionism was the big problem in this pattern. You struggled with divine discontent, meaning that no matter what you did, it was just not good enough. You talked yourself out of a goal before it was completed because you feared the finished product would not be good enough. There were times you went all the way to the end of a plan and then scrapped it, thinking it wasn't perfect enough. You too often grew disappointed in others because they could not live up to the high standards you set for them. You had wonderful ideals but needed more internal strength and stability to be happy.

Sneak Attack

When you were angry at someone, you often did not use a direct confrontation. Instead, you tried to sabotage their plans in a sneaky way. You were good at concealing your motives, but hidden intentions eventually backfired, making you unpopular. You alienated close friends and loved ones by not being honest with them. Your insecurity was at the root of this pattern. You were not an open person when it came to feelings. This was a passive-aggressive type of behavior to manipulate others. Your lack of trust didn't help matters, and having the faith to be honest in communication was lacking.

Hypnotized

In some incarnations, you became too addicted to people. Your dependency needs were way out of alignment. Your whole life was too focused on making someone else happy, forgetting your own needs in the process. Your reality-testing was way off-center. You saw beautiful things in others that they just couldn't live up to. A tendency to overly idealize your lovers was the problem. Your own goals were too easily sacrificed in order to give all of your energy to someone else. Low self-esteem was often the culprit in this pattern. You didn't have the fulfillment you really wanted with your relationships being so out of balance.

Illumination for the Current Life

If these past-life patterns are a recurring problem in the current life, there are ways to make amends with them. It will take consistent effort to get better mileage out of your energy, but you can convert these old negative behaviors into positive expressions.

The Waterlogged pattern requires that you have more faith in yourself, which can neutralize guilt. When you allow guilt to be the cause of your actions, it turns out to be counterproductive. Your momentum comes to a standstill if you can't untangle yourself from emotional confusion. Trusting your instincts more and following through on your goals helps clear the air. Defining clearer boundaries points you in the right direction. You have to be grounded to clearly feel your way out of the emotional confusion. It may be that you need distance from people who are too critical and who cause you to be in a confused mental state. You have a powerful intuition that can give you inner strength to get beyond this pattern. Keep nurturing your intuitive energy and it will come through for you!

For the Idealism Lost rut, you need to be more reasonable in terms of perfection. Don't make your goals so lofty that you can never realize them. Keep it simple. If you see others more realistically, it brings balance to your relationships. It's fine to have ideals—they inspire you—just be sure to make your goals attainable. It takes practice to know when to stop perfecting a plan. It's okay to make mistakes! It takes a lot of pressure off of you if you will allow for errors; they are part of life and you can learn from them. It's better to keep moving forward toward your ambitions and not worry so much about every detail along the way. Your intuitive energy can help guide you to clarity. You may need to take more time to reflect and tune into your inner strength. Then again, taking a creative risk pushes you forward and lets you see that you have more potential than you realize.

The Sneak Attack pattern needs you to be direct in expressing your intentions. Your anger gets out of proportion to the problem when you keep it hidden. Your relationships are closer and more fulfilling when you take an honest approach to communication. It does take trust and a great belief in your own ability to talk things out with others. Holding back your anger is not good for your mental or physical health. You will find greater energy if you learn to talk straight. Rather than sabotaging someone's goals, it is far better to let them know how you feel. There will be greater harmony and love in your life when you adopt a win-win strategy.

The Hypnotized routine is conquered through not giving away your power so easily. The attributes you are so compulsively seeking in a lover are already within you. Projecting your finest qualities onto someone else (and away from yourself) takes away from your own potential. Your self-esteem needs to rise. The best way to do this is by fulfilling some of your own goals. Keep reminding yourself that you are already a whole person, so nobody can truly "complete" you. There are no perfect people. Breaking an addictive pattern takes a lot of determination. With regular effort you can do this. It helps to have good friends who help keep you away from individuals looking to take advantage of you. You need as many positive affirmations as possible and regular reminders to stay clear of people who keep you from realizing your true potential.

RoadMap to Your Empowerment

The Second Zone of Scorpio is a highly intuitive place, filling you with an endless amount of imagination. This is the kind of terrain where dreams form quickly, having Pisces as your zone ruler. Channeling your emotions into creative power comes as you get grounded and achieve self-mastery. *The key to your personal empowerment is trusting your intuition and giving it a solid foundation to rest upon.* Your ideals inspire you, as do your causes. Maintaining a clear sense of direction comes when you learn how to reality-test your idealism.

Finding a profession that captures your passion is an innate yearning. Romance fuels your creative drive and enlivens your purpose. Defining your dependency needs clearly keeps you focused and fulfilled. Trying to attain perfection may deepen your life purpose, but you are happier when you realize that the world is imperfect and so are people. Keeping your expectations of self and others reasonable points the way to harmony. Your willpower is stronger when you believe in your capability. You attain a spiritual, mental, and physical balance when you first look within yourself for happiness. There is no end to the self-discovery you can find in this birth zone that offers endless intuitive insights.

Third Zone of Scorpio: **11/11–11/20**
Element: **Water**
Third Zone Sign Ruler: **Cancer**
Third Zone Energy Field: **Cardinal**
Third Zone Signs: **Scorpio plus Cancer = Passionate Emotions**

Current Life Scan for the Scorpio Third Zone

Your soul longed for an opportunity to explore the mysteries of life and to establish a clear intuitive understanding of how the world operates. Being born in the Third Zone of Scorpio indicates you have strong emotions that need to be carefully channeled in the right directions. You don't like to do a job halfway unless it stops inspiring you. *A primary drive is to find passionate goals for your creative intensity.* Finding a lifestyle that makes you feel secure is a lifelong pursuit.

Understanding your inner motivations for actions makes your life run smoother. You don't like letting people make decisions for you. Finding equality in your partnerships is highly valued. Trust does not come easy for you. Feeling safe with a lover is the ticket to a deeper loyalty. Keeping your dependency needs balanced ensures your freedom and happiness.

Your moods are powerful. They help you tune into the pulse of situations. Expressing anger is better than holding it in. You maintain longer commitments from friends and lovers when you don't take your frustrations out on them. Being true to your dreams keeps you feeling alive and energized. You often think about the past, trying to process what those experiences meant. When you are able make peace with your past, your eyes look with great anticipation of fulfillment into the present and future. You experience rebirth when finding those paths that let your intuition speak loudly and allow your mind to feel nurtured with new experiences.

Past-Life Patterns for the Scorpio Third Zone

Your past-life issues were associated with three themes. One was *unpredictable moods* that came on quickly and produced impulsive behaviors. A second area was *hidden anger*, which caused you to be more combative than needed. A third trend was *emotional confusion*, causing you to become mentally fogged. You did not always act out these patterns but when you did, your life lacked balance and happiness.

Introspector

Sometimes you had a tendency to look too deeply within for too long! You overanalyzed your feelings. This kept you worrying over past situations that should have been long forgotten. You were too obsessed with fixing what could not be resolved, and you kept going over these circumstances in your head. You could be too withdrawn and quiet. It was difficult to get you to talk out your worries. You took privacy too far, in that you built walls around yourself. Keeping too many secrets caused confusion and unclear communication in your relationships. You became so detached that people weren't sure how to connect with you. A stubborn unwillingness to reveal your inner world contributed to the problem.

Vindictive Venom

In some incarnations, you were too jealous of others. You kept your anger bottled up until it eventually exploded. This took a toll on your mental and physical health. You didn't enjoy your relationships as much as you could have. Sudden angry outbursts caused instability in your everyday living. There was a tendency to sabotage your partnerships because you didn't have faith that they could be successful. Your self-esteem was low and was often the source of this pattern. An addiction to negative thinking kept you inside of this behavior. Your mind was poisoned by an unwillingness to dream of a better life.

Mood Swings

Your emotions went on a roller coaster ride at times, taking you along for a wild excursion. You didn't like losing control and the harder you tried to reign in your emotions, the worse it got. You tended to worry too much about the outcome of situations, which was one reason this pattern manifested. There were times when you didn't know how to get grounded. Self-criticism was perhaps the biggest cause of this problem. You didn't like yourself enough. Your intuition was powerful and tried to guide you out of harm's way, but you were not calm enough to get it to work for you. Receiving nurturing energy was not easy. You resisted people who tried to help ease your mind. Being a loner and wanting to tough it out on your own only prolonged your difficulty in finding peace.

Cold War

You could be quiet one minute and at war the next. You plotted your moves carefully before attacking. People got more worried the quieter you became, fearing you were getting ready to strike. You were in the habit of giving someone the silent treatment for long periods of time when angry. This did push people away from you. You did brood and stew for long periods of time over differences with others. You didn't trust people very easily, which was one of the big reasons for this pattern. You had trouble being in touch with your emotions. There were occasions when you were too sensitive to criticism, perceiving it as a personal attack. An inability to negotiate openly kept you from relationship success.

Illumination for the Current Life

If these past-life patterns are once again active in your life, there are ways to conquer them. You will need to stay persistent in turning them into positive expressions. The key is to be patient and determined to overcome their influences.

With the Introspector habit, you need to become more intimate and trusting of your inner world. It's okay to share some of your secrets with others—it might actually be one of the best ways to stop obsessing over the past. There are some things you can't change, and you spend a lot of energy dwelling over and over again on your worries.

You will have much more productivity and happiness when you learn to release the past. You have a great capacity to process in your birth zone. Both Scorpio and your zone ruler, Cancer, are wonderful signs for breaking the hold of concerns that wear you down. You will be perceived as a warmer person when you communicate feelings. Your relationships and professional life will prosper if you start to go with life's flow. Trust your intuition—it can point the way to a clearer path in not focusing on unnecessary worry.

The Vindictive Venom pattern can be converted into a positive expression by trusting that it is good to talk through your feelings, even your resentful ones. When you hold back your anger, it builds to such an extreme that it comes out in a convoluted manner. Your relationships bear the brunt of this negative energy, destabilizing them. Your mental, emotional, and physical well-being improve immensely when you are direct in venting your intensity. It's difficult to get a gauge on your feelings if you never talk about them. When your inner world stays a mystery, it tends to cause great distance between you and those you truly care about. Your self-esteem may need work. It's vital that you value yourself. Why? Because it is the surest way to gain insight about this pattern: self-worth elevates your consciousness to a high enough plateau to get the perspective you require. A healthy self-esteem can dissipate the emotional cloud obscuring your clarity and can entice you into honest dialogue with others.

The Mood Swings pattern requires you to worry less and not indulge as much in self-criticism. It could be that nobody will be harder on you than *you!* If this is true, you need to cultivate positive thinking. That's the medicine to heal this old nemesis. You will have more consistency and follow-through if you get this pattern under wraps. It's not possible to be in control of your feelings all of the time. If you clamp down too hard on your emotional side, you are working against yourself. Your creative power moves through you in big waves when you relax into your self-expression. Receive help when it's offered by those trying to be supportive. Such support could be the catalyst to get you out of this pattern. Learning to tune into your intuition may save you time and energy. Meditating and reflecting can help you process. If you are a very restless type, physical exercise or projects could be just the thing to work off your inner anxiety levels. The idea is to stabilize this ocean of emotion constantly circulating through your consciousness.

Ending the Cold War requires that you be less calculating in your every move. Allow for a bit of spontaneity. Trust is essential to overcoming this pattern. Having the faith that you can openly discuss matters with others goes far. A desire for quiet time comes naturally for you being born in this sign zone. Water people like yourself need space to process and get refueled. However, if you grow too secretive, it creates mistrust in the people you are trying to get close to. There is a proper time for hiding your intentions—you don't have to trust *everyone*. Just be sure to reveal enough of your inner world to your favorite friends, family, and lovers. Nobody likes to be criticized, and if you are in the company of negative individuals too much of the time, you may need to distance yourself from them. Being around people who make you feel safe and valued could alleviate the need to repeat this pattern.

RoadMap to Your Empowerment

The Third Zone of Scorpio is a vast terrain to explore your inner world in the deepest of ways. You are blessed with a powerful intuition. Gaining understanding of your inner motivations helps clear your path to happiness. *The key to your personal empowerment is having faith in your insights and the courage to adjust your goals when needed.* Trusting your ability to get to know others on deep, intimate levels comes with time. Learning to discriminate what types of individuals are good to have as friends and lovers ensures emotional stability.

Your self-mastery comes through having faith in your ability. You must have a high sense of self-worth to be successful, as this gives you the strength to make the right choices. You do better when not focusing too much on the past. You have an innate talent to process life experiences and their impact on you, but it's just as important to realize your impact on others. You enjoy people who make you feel safe and valued. When you negotiate honestly with others, your partnerships blossom. Showing the world your knowledge expands your horizons. New challenges stimulate you to feel more vitality. You like to stay in your comfort zones. Routines are okay—just don't forget to venture out and see more of what the world has to offer. This keeps your mind curious and your heart beating more lively.

Sagittarius: The Explorer

11/21-12/20

Traditional Astrology Phrase: "I Understand"
Archetypal Theme: Self-Expressive Discovery

First Zone of Sagittarius: **11/21–11/30**
Element: **Fire**
First Zone Sign Ruler: **Sagittarius**
First Zone Energy Field: **Mutable**
First Zone Signs: **Sagittarius plus Sagittarius =**
Expansive Quest for Meaning

Current Life Scan for the Sagittarius First Zone

Your soul entered this life with a fiery zeal. Being born in the First
Zone of Sagittarius lights your eyes with "truth oil." Finding exciting
paths to launch your enthusiasm is highly desired. Your ideals are your
guiding light through emotional storms, when your vision is obscured
by mental fog. You prefer to have a lot on your plate to keep you from
growing bored.

A primary drive is to seek knowledge in order to deepen your awareness
of the world around you. The four corners of the globe feel like they
beckon you to explore them. You thirst for new learning. Many perceive you to be a student, gypsy, and philosopher. Highly refined communication skills make you a natural teacher, advisor, and consultant.
Variety is your middle name. An inner restlessness drives you to create
and to act on impulse.

Taking risks is soul-felt, although your lovers, family, and friends
may wish you weren't so adventurous. When you find focus, your skill
levels improve immensely. You will honor commitments that seem to
have integrity and capture your imagination. There are times you are
too changeable and don't finish what you start. Your sense of humor
endears you to others. Discovering how to make use of reality-testing
saves you time, money, and heartache. Your heart is big and quite generous. You probably never met a stranger, as people quickly sense that
you understand them. It's your positive attitude that opens the doors
to happiness and success.

Past-Life Patterns for the Sagittarius First Zone

Your past-life issues were connected to four themes. One was being *overly expansive*; you did not get focused very easily. A second was being *too passive*, always seeking the path of least resistance. Another area was being *extremely opinionated*. A fourth trend was *escapism*; running away seemed like the answer. When you were involved with these patterns, your life lacked balance and stability.

All Roads Lead to Rome

You liked to travel several different paths at once. It was fun to entertain yourself this way but not very productive. Completing a plan was a challenge because your concentration was weak. The focus was missing. You eventually frustrated yourself and those who depended on you. It was your expansive mind, which wanted to experience life from all sorts of directions, that got you into this pattern. Exhaustion—mental and physical—frequently wore you down. Your work and relationships bore the brunt of this behavior. People didn't trust that you could finish what you set out to accomplish. Chasing after more than one cause at a time with good intentions often confused you. Your ideals lacked the reality-testing that could have put you on a path to harmony.

Avoiding Conflict

This pattern surfaced when you could not face adversity. You preferred to be in denial, ignoring everything that didn't fit nicely into place. This caused you to miss out on opportunities that could have resulted in success with only a little effort. Your creative intensity was weaker than it could have been. Your passion for life was dulled by seeking the easy way out. Relationships ended abruptly when you ran from problems. You were very idealistic and thought people needed to be perfect to fit into your world. Messy situations either scared or annoyed you. Being free of the entanglements that serious commitments caused was your preference. You had a lot of unfinished business, which kept your life in a constant state of crisis.

Grass is Greener

When escapism was your passion, you didn't follow through on commitments. You thought your problems would disappear if you went where the grass seemed greener. Denial caused you to remain in this behavior far too long. What you were running from followed you from one place to another. Your internal struggles were usually the source of the issue. An unclear identity was what pushed you to keep this pattern going, and being on the run from yourself was really the bottom line. Facing your shortcomings was not in the game plan. You put off dealing with problems until they grew too big to fix. You had an overly idealistic lens in some incarnations, which made facing reality difficult.

Judge and Jury

Being too judgmental alienated friends and lovers. If you became too dogmatic, it caused this pattern to surface. You felt like you had the only truth. Not listening to the opinions of others caused great tension in your relationships. When you came across as the judge, it distanced you from those you wanted to come closer. Your rush to judgment was a fast impulse that caused unnecessary disputes. Power struggles resulted from refusing to consider someone else's point of view. Impatience contributed to this behavior. You tended to have a dogmatic vision that was too self-serving.

Illumination for the Current Life

If any of these past-life patterns of the Sagittarius First Zone are active once again in your present life, there are ways to navigate successfully through their influences. It will take regular effort and patience to overcome them.

To neutralize the All Roads Lead to Rome tendency, you need to try keeping your life simpler. Too many targets cause you to lose your focus. There is a natural exploring tendency in your zone that can push you to be overly expansive. More is not necessarily better; think quality over quantity. You will get more accomplished by finishing one plan and then starting on another. (Or at least try keeping to just two or three paths simultaneously.) Your friends, family, lovers, and work colleagues will be less frustrated with you when they see you as a better closer. The adventurous spirit you were born with by virtue of this highly energized zone will always give you restless tendencies. Channeling this passion with greater awareness will yield better results. You have an eclectic mind, meaning you like to get your knowledge from more than one source. That's fine—just be sure not to overfill your plate to the point of confusion. Staying organized is a challenge you can learn to handle. When you manage your time and schedule responsibly, the world loves you!

Facing conflict more directly puts the Avoiding Conflict pattern in its place. Your birth zone will entice you at times to see dealing with problems as a waste of time. When you do take on serious challenges, your inner strength multiplies and your creative power increases. Your relationships deepen in commitment if you stay and work out the issues. There is no use in looking for perfect people—they don't exist. But you can create relationships that meet your needs by dealing with your differences. New opportunities present themselves when you are willing to look them in the eyes. A deeper purpose is discovered through not running from adversity. Life can become messy and very emotional. When you don't let your fears cause you to leave good situations too quickly, new options are possible. You develop deeper insights by staying the course and marching through obstacles.

The Grass is Greener attitude requires that you not look to simply start over when the going gets tough. Tuning into your inner world is the best way out of this maze. Otherwise your inner strife will keep you thinking that the grass truly is greener elsewhere. You can plant new grass right where you live! It's true that you were born into a great sign zone for reinventing yourself from time to time, but you can't do this constantly or you will lose your bearings. Having ideals is wonderful and you probably have several. Reality-testing your goals and thoughts keeps you on the straight and narrow. You are a restless type. Sagittarius is known as the archer, and you will shoot those arrows at the distant horizon, hoping it holds the answers you seek. Remember not to lose sight of the demands of the here and now. You are much stronger internally than you realize. Testing your ability to finish what you start is wise. You gain clarity with discipline.

The Judge and Jury habit can be overcome by being tolerant of opposing viewpoints. Agreeing to disagree will sometimes be the wisest policy. You aren't meant to win every argument, even though you may feel you have the better solution. Giving others the freedom to speak their own minds makes them become your true friends and allies. Your relationships will gain stability and clarity with open dialogue. You can still be the fiery passionate soul that inhabits your body. Nobody will ever take that away. Broadening your perspective so that there is room enough for shared ideas brings you closer to harmony. Your values are fine to uphold. When you show respect for those of someone else, it lessens any tension between you. Keep that sense of humor handy—it allows you to step back and see a bigger picture and a more peaceful reality!

RoadMap to Your Empowerment

The First Zone of Sagittarius is a speedy terrain, accelerating your impulse to take creative risks. You are apt to seek new information in many exciting ways. You like to know there are options to any plan you endorse. *The key to your personal empowerment is keeping an open mind when confronted by contradicting ideas and having the faith to be true to your ideals.* You are at your best when reality-checking your goals to ensure they are based on sound logic.

Not setting off into too many directions at once helps you maintain a clear mind. There will be endless temptation to try multiple paths in search of the right creative fit for your eager imagination. You were born in one of the most idealistic sign zones. In many ways you are a true romantic, and falling in love with life keeps you inspired.

You need stimulating growth opportunities to keep you alert. When you stay clear of procrastination, your life is more rewarding.

Cultivating an optimistic philosophy opens doors. Overconfidence is not your ally. Being reasonable in your expectations keeps you humble and ready to act on inventive insights. You excel when engaging in activities that express a competitive spirit along with an open heart.

Second Zone of Sagittarius: **12/1–12/10**
Element: **Fire**
Second Zone Sign Ruler: **Aries**
Second Zone Energy Field: **Cardinal**
Second Zone Signs: **Sagittarius plus Aries = Sudden Energy Bursts**

Current Life Scan for the Sagittarius Second Zone

Your soul sensed this was going to be a lifetime filled with excitement, indicated by being born into the action-packed Second Zone of Sagittarius. An innate love of adventure colors your mental impulses. You prefer not having days that repeat one after the other with the same schedule. However, you are willing to endure routines if there is a reward for doing so. Stimulation through travel and encountering new challenges is what you like.

A primary drive is a quest for invigorating challenges that are catalysts for growth. You tend to have strong opinions about your favorite subjects. It's important that you become a good listener so you can be more open to different perspectives. Your life goes more smoothly when you agree to compromise. Keeping a sense of humor helps you not to take your own ideas too seriously.

Learning to follow through on commitments solidifies your partnerships. You prefer a profession that allows you to communicate vivaciously. Your work has to be able to capture your imagination or you may lose focus. You are attracted to individuals with outgoing personalities and who have similar values.

Past-Life Patterns for the Sagittarius Second Zone

The past-life issues were linked to four themes. One was too much *self-focus*; you were not interested in the needs of others. Another area was *dogmatism*, when you pushed your ideas intensely. A third trend was *missing the details*, caused by an inner restlessness. The fourth was a *lack of commitment*. You did not always act out these patterns. But when you did, life was out of balance.

Arrogant Individualist

You fought for your own ideas at times without considering the impact on others. When you became overly aggressive, it caused great tension in all of your relationships. Power struggles occurred regularly. A strong desire to be the center of attention did anger people. You liked to argue as a way of wearing down people in order to get your own way. Your actions were often unpredictable because you liked to be spontaneous. You were perceived as unreliable when you left work undone. Being a team member was not part of your plan. An aloof personality distanced you from others. Your inner world was not easily shared with anyone. Life grew lonely when you chose paths that were too full of self-gain.

My Way Is the Only Way

This pattern found you preaching narrow views that refused to make enough room for the opinions of others. You forcefully pushed your ideas on others. An extreme attachment to your own belief system angered those not agreeing with you. Your intolerance caused distance with others. You were so sure your truths were good for all that you closed your mind to new information. Arguing your philosophy was a regular way of life. You became judgmental, which didn't endear you to family, lovers, and friends. You had a tunnel vision that only chose to acknowledge reality from a very narrow lens. You missed out on opportunities for growth and greater abundance by confining your world to a restricted set of beliefs.

Not Seeing the Trees for the Forest

You moved so fast that you skipped right over the details in some past lives. Patience was not one of your strong points. You were in such a hurry to get to the next step that you liked to jump right to the finish line. Your friends and lovers didn't exactly like it when you rushed through life. You lost money and time by not caring about the small facts, which usually came back later to bite you. You liked looking at the big picture but tended to ignore those nagging little details too much of the time. Having to do things over again due to not paying enough attention to your immediate surroundings proved frustrating.

Rolling Stone

It is an understatement to say you were a gypsy type of traveler, but that in itself was not the problem. It was when you lacked any desire for stability that your life sometimes became unglued. Your commitment to deal with a challenge wasn't very strong. Escapism was at the root of this pattern. Running away from responsibility made people mad at you. Your creative potential went unrealized because you had no true focus. You were often very talented but needed to plant some roots and find your footing. Future goals were seen as day-to-day living. Long-term relationships fell apart due to constantly being on the move. You were ruled by an inner restlessness that was not under control.

Illumination for the Current Life

If these Sagittarius Second Zone patterns are once again a problem in this incarnation, there are methods for making them friendlier. It will take regular effort to get more positive results. With practice and patience, you can be successful in getting past these behaviors.

The Arrogant Individualist can win more friends and create fewer adversaries by being more inclusive of the ideas of others. Taking some of the attention off of you and paying greater attention to what other people need wins you cooperation. Fewer power struggles and greater harmony in your relationships is the payoff. It's okay to have spontaneity; however, clueing someone in to your plan will keep them on the same page. You build trust through clearer communication. Your uniqueness does not need to be sacrificed—just a few compromises will go a long way in getting people to believe in you. Treating others as equals brings peace and love into your life. Showing support for someone's goals will get them on your side when you might need a friend.

The My Way Is the Only Way trend calls for you to open your world. The stimulation of different views helps you grow. When you let go of your fear of other truths, your mind broadens in perspective. There is less tension in your exchange of ideas when you tolerate differences. You were born into a sign zone that is eclectic in nature, which encourages you to go beyond one belief system. The more you drink from multiple fountains of knowledge, the better off you will be. Your luck and good fortune are enhanced when you embrace information from several sources. Letting your mind explore universal truths leads you to great self-discovery. You will find people are willing listeners if you are one as well. An open dialogue enlarges your vision of the future and fills your life with creative possibilities.

The Not Seeing the Trees for the Forest problem requires that you slow down and notice more of what is going on around you. Being more aware of details might save you some aggravation later. Your birth zone has a natural push to look at large perspectives. Dreaming big is okay, but don't forget the little steps needed to put that plan into motion. Your friends and lovers will like you more if you gain a keener awareness of the things needed to ensure a plan will be a success. Your profession and daily responsibilities benefit if you take the extra time to go over the finished product to make sure you didn't leave anything out before moving on to the next project.

There is nothing wrong with being an explorer, but even a Rolling Stone needs to have some degree of being grounded. Why? It will help you tune into your creative power. Being on the move can be very exciting and stimulating. Travel and adventure keep you young and energetic. But if you are running from problems, it is better to deal with them. You will have greater energy and clarity, as well as peace of mind. Everyone indulges in some escapism. If you are seeking to escape from responsibility too often, it takes away from the continuity you need to reach your goals. Your relationships and work are stabilized when you follow through on commitments. So be that gypsy and student of life! Just be sure to stop long enough to smell the roses and to connect with a deeper sense of self-discovery.

Your RoadMap to Empowerment

The Second Zone of Sagittarius is a terrain filled with sudden adventurous impulses. Being born in this zone pushes you to act boldly. *The key to your personal empowerment is developing the insight to time your actions so as to get the best results.* You can be a trailblazer and inventor of new trends. Your zeal to learn inspires others to grow. Staying open to new perspectives enlarges your growth potential.

Channeling your inner restlessness helps fulfill your goals. You thrive on competition. Defending your ideas is a natural instinct. Treating others as equals makes for harmony. Be assertive rather than aggressive. You have charisma when communicating in a lively manner and with a sense of the impact of your words.

You create your own luck when you have faith in your ideals. Doors open when you follow through on your commitments. Learn from the past, face the present with eager eyes, and look to the future with a desire to expand your understanding. You don't have all of the answers. Then again, nobody really does. It's in sharing your wealth of life experiences that others learn to admire you. Your inner world is strengthened when you express a few of your secrets. The love and abundance you seek are usually only a positive thought away. It's okay to make mistakes. Just remember not to dwell on them and your path will never lose its way toward fulfilling directions. Balancing your need to see the details with maintaining a long-range vision keeps you centered and happy.

Third Zone of Sagittarius: **12/11–12/20**
Element: **Fire**
Third Zone Sign Ruler: **Leo**
Third Zone Energy Field: **Fixed**
Third Zone Signs: **Sagittarius plus Leo =**
Falling In Love with Creativity

Current Life Scan for the Sagittarius Third Zone

Your soul entered this incarnation with a playful spirit. Being born in the Third Zone of Sagittarius shows that a passion for displaying your abilities started early. You can be the center of attention without even trying. Acting out roles that best fit your personality is exhilarating. You make a good leader, as your enthusiasm can be contagious. Being a cheerleader for those you care about makes you popular. Your emotions can be intense and need to be aimed productively. *A primary drive is finding outlets for your creative passion.* Having the ego strength to show your talent to the world is a must. You need to watch out for overconfidence. Knowing your limits is just as vital as having self-confidence. Finding a happy medium between the two keeps you centered and happy.

You are attracted to outgoing people. Sharing the spotlight with others keeps your relationships balanced. Being an equal in your partnerships is required for you to feel there is enough room to discover your own true potential.

Teaching and advising come naturally to you. Even selling ideas and products are within your grasp. You are a high-energy person and need plenty of activities to work off nervous energy. Learning patience helps you clarify your goals. Your insights deepen when you don't fear taking advantage of a new opportunity. Self-mastery comes when you are able to adapt to change. Having an equal exchange of giving and receiving keeps your life moving in a fulfilling direction.

Past-Life Patterns for the Sagittarius Third Zone

The past-life issues for you were connected to four themes. One was *overconfidence*; you thought you just could not lose. Another was *feeling too entitled*, when you expected things to come with no effort. A third was being *too competitive*; you did not know when to stop pushing for what you wanted. A fourth was *low self-esteem*. When you fell into these behaviors, life was not as rewarding.

I Can't Possibly Lose

There were past lives where you had so much confidence that you forgot to heed the warnings that you were pushing your limits. Your resistance to listening to good advice was very strong. You liked to be your own person and take risks just to test the odds, even if they were stacked heavily against you. Your enjoyment of living on the edge is often what got you into trouble. You weren't worried about saving for a rainy day, as the old saying goes. Living in the fast lane turned you on. The adrenaline rush is what you enjoyed. Your mind didn't consider slowing down and thinking about the consequences of your actions. Being ruled by sudden impulses got you into fast trouble too many times. An all-or-nothing philosophy sometimes left you with nothing.

Serve Me on a Silver Platter

There were times you waited for life to give you what you desired, thinking it would come without putting out any energy. A sense of entitlement found you waiting for others to open the door of opportunity for you. Your goals grew stale when your mind became stagnant. Waiting around for things to work in your favor often didn't manifest abundance. The source of this pattern was dwelling on negative thinking. It kept you stuck. Another trend was being a procrastinator. You waited until the last minute to see if someone else would make the effort for you. You had a dynamic energy but hesitated in putting your best foot forward. There were lives that showed you fearing failure. This caused you to lack the assertiveness to put your ideas into motion.

Winning at All Costs

If you got competitive beyond reason, you fell into this pattern. You were not sympathetic to the loser. Your drive to be a success became all-consuming. It's what made you get up every day. This didn't make people want to be close to you. Your mind was on material gain to such an extreme that your emotional world felt the fallout. You often felt very alone in the world, since your winnings didn't prove comforting when you needed a shoulder to lean on. You had few friends because what you valued was more in terms of dollars and cents. You didn't always have a real good gauge on reality when taking risky chances. Power struggles occurred because you tended to force people to be on the defensive.

Fixation on Limitation

Your self-esteem got too low in some incarnations. It caused you to accent the negative, which didn't get good results. You stayed in limiting relationships and work situations far beyond their fulfillment points. You bought into criticism too easily. You surrendered your power without much of a fight. Your identity depended too much on what others thought of you. When you idealized others too much, your own needs often were neglected. Trying to make others like you caused you to be a person you were not. You lacked abundance consciousness. Your thoughts focused on what you could not accomplish more than on what you could accomplish. Believing in individuals who didn't return the favor left you in limiting circumstances.

Illumination for the Current Life

If these patterns of the Sagittarius Third Zone are a problem in this incarnation, you can get past their influences. It will take regular attentiveness and patience to accomplish your objectives. These patterns don't have to be a repeat performance. It will take persistence, but you can do it!

With the I Can't Possibly Lose trait, you need to slow down and take a good look before leaping into a risky situation. With twenty-twenty hindsight, you probably will wish you had not jumped blindly. Your sign zone fills you with a spirit that enjoys crossing beyond comfort zones. It's what makes you an inspirational force to many. Being an optimistic Sagittarius, with a bold Leo sign zone ruler at your side, pushes you to climb to new heights. Ambition is fine. Taking well-calculated risks is in your DNA. However, staying realistic in your assessment of your ability saves you a lot of time, energy, and pain. Your love life and financial well-being will stay in great shape if you learn your limits. You are blessed with dynamic energy being born in this zone. All it takes to be happy and successful is reflecting a bit more before taking action.

The Serve Me on a Silver Platter trap needs some of your sign zone ruler Leo's initiating energy to get you moving forward boldly toward your objectives. If negative thoughts hold you back, you need to latch onto Leo's boldness and Sagittarius' positive mind-set to turn your life around. You have the power to make your own good luck. Your attraction power is a hot item—let it work for you! Let your creative passion put your life into motion. There is no reason to sit back and wait when you have this kind of gusto working for you all of the time. It does take your first step of effort to ignite it. You are at your best when not waiting for permission to embark in a new direction. Don't fear making a mistake. Everyone makes them; it is part of learning how to do something better. Keep a sense of humor and have fun with the process of creating a fulfilling future.

The Winning at All Costs tendency can be overcome by toning down the need to always come in first. When you are supportive of others, your relationships find balance. Power struggles become less likely when you negotiate fairly. You have a wonderful competitive spirit. When used wisely, your assertiveness sees goals accomplished. It's fine to make money and achieve, but you need to widen your perspective and include other life pursuits. Paying more attention to your emotional needs leads to inner fulfillment. The material world can only offer so much, as it has its limitations. Focus as much on building friendships as you do championing your own causes. Balancing your material aims with spiritual and emotional needs gives you a greater sense of unity. You will attract more of what you need if you develop your intuitive side.

The Fixation on Limitation pattern is conquered by training your mind to think more positively. You may need to steer clear of individuals who negate your goals. Building your self-esteem is a must. Valuing your own needs is a first powerful step in the right direction. Reclaiming your power comes through having the faith to leave limiting relationships and jobs. You need to visualize situations that show you in far better circumstances—circumstances that offer the kind of life you want to have. Self-criticism needs to be replaced with good thoughts about your potential. Fixating on abundance neutralizes this rut of being confined to whatever is holding you back. It's time to move into a new role in the play of life, one that releases your creative power!

RoadMap to Your Empowerment

The Third Zone of Sagittarius is a highly energized terrain that can fire your brain synapses to new insights. Being born in this confidence-producing land can help you reinvent yourself in a flash. *The key to your personal empowerment is allowing yourself to be swept up by new life paths that offer you a deeper sense of identity.* Developing your intuition is just as important as carving out material niches in the world. You have an endless amount of energy that needs to be channeled carefully to get the most out of your actions.

Relationships that stimulate you to be inventive are rewarding. Remember to give to others as much as you receive, and you will establish harmony. You have a tendency to want life to be on your own terms, as your sign zone ruler Leo is a Fixed sign. This shows you have more follow-through than the other two Sagittarius sign zones, but it also means you need to find flexibility to ensure success.

You like to think about the future. The romantic and dreamer within you loves to dance freely with few strings attached. Honoring your commitments builds trust. Honest communication deepens your bond with others. You like falling in love with a special partner and with a chosen profession. Remember to keep falling in love with what you cherish, over and over again, and there will be longevity. Admit when you are wrong and people will come closer. Standing up for your values strengthens your inner world. Staying aware of what your most intimate friends need keeps your heart warm and fulfilled.

Capricorn: The Pragmatist

12/21-1/19

Traditional Astrology Phrase: "I Build"
Archetypal Theme: Desire for Success

First Zone of Capricorn: **12/21–12/30**
Element: **Earth**
First Zone Sign Ruler: **Capricorn**
First Zone Energy Field: **Cardinal**
First Zone Signs: **Capricorn plus Capricorn = Incredible Focus**

Current Life Scan for the Capricorn First Zone

Your soul knew this was going to be a life in which to get a lot accomplished in a very focused way. Being born in the First Zone of Capricorn shows you to be a solid planner when you want to be. Your choices need to be carefully considered because you have the instinct to commit seriously to your goals. Learning to be flexible helps you to adjust to changes. Ambition flows through your mind quickly when you become inspired to make a dream come true.

A primary drive is initiating life directions that are large enough to satisfy your passion to build safe and reliable creative expressions. You detest failing at anything you want to accomplish. Learning to accept your shortcomings is as important as celebrating your milestones. Keeping a sober attitude about success keeps you happier. Accepting life's ups and downs gives you a sense of inner peace.

You like people with well-conceived ideas. Idealists appeal to you if they can prove they have a firm grasp of reality. You are a pragmatist at heart with a love of pleasurable escapes. Finding hobbies and other pastimes to relieve your anxieties about life adds to your mental and physical health. Seeing the cup as at least half full helps you maintain a positive outlook. You are a "show me" type of person who wants others to convince you of their value in your life. People perceive you as generous when your heart is open to sharing your knowledge and resources. You prefer lovers and friends who are able to accept you just the way you are. Your life blossoms when you bypass your fears and pursue the ideals that motivate your innermost world. Happiness with a profession is more likely when you grow comfortable with your ability. You need a stable family or private life to balance the intensity you naturally pour into your outer world in search of success.

Past-Life Patterns for the Capricorn First Zone

The past-life issues for you were connected to three themes. One was *extreme ambition drives*; you got carried away in becoming a big success. A second was being *too rigid*; adaptability was not a strong suit. The last one was being *too defensive*. This isn't saying you always acted out these traits. When you did, life was not as fulfilling.

Climbing the Ladder of Success

It wasn't a bad thing that you often found professional outlets that matched your talent. That was the good news. It was your absolute determination to be a winner no matter what you had to do to get there that got you into trouble. Sacrificing your relationships was not uncommon. You put huge amounts of time into building careers and businesses. You lost awareness of those important friends, relatives, and lovers who helped you get to the top. You had a cold logic that didn't warm the hearts of those who cared about your emotional well-being. Your ambition is what drove you, ruling your everyday thinking. Your focusing power was tremendous but usually limited to work and making money. Your world was confined to putting all of your energy into getting ahead. Materially you often out-distanced the competition. When you did lose after taking a risk, you didn't have a great personal life to fall back on. You limited your options to a world of wealth-seeking and excluded other alternatives for fulfillment. You lacked openness to a wider perspective that could have rounded out your days in a much more satisfying way.

I Am the Boss

A compulsive need to be in control did occur in some lives. Things had to be done your way or they were seen as incorrect. You had very high expectations of others. You became downright demanding. A strict adherence to rules and routines was your formula for life. You liked being a leader, and it was your bossiness that irritated others. Arguments ensued from those who resisted your dominance. You did become obstinate when your authority was challenged. There was an inability to delegate responsibility because an underlying current in this pattern was a lack of trust for others. You didn't feel they could do a job as well as you could. There was a side of you that was very attached to overpowering people. Another force at work was hiding your insecurity or fears by acting all-powerful. You missed out on closeness and a richer emotional life by hiding behind a false persona of not needing anyone. Life grew pretty lonely. You suffered in silence.

The Tree That Would Not Bend

Inflexibility caused you to be fixated on repeating the same mistakes, despite their bad results. A refusal to adapt to new situations caused you to miss out on opportunities for abundance. Even if your actions were the catalyst for emotional storms in your life, you insisted on forcing the same agendas. Emotional and nervous breakdowns occurred because you lacked the insight to see your way out of situations. You needed to invent a whole new script for yourself but would not start writing one. People had to fit into the game you were playing. Holding onto worn-out ideas kept you lagging behind when it came to getting ahead in life. Change scared you. The more you held onto the past, the worse it got for you.

On My Guard

You could be a tough nut to crack emotionally. Your feelings were well-insulated from others. You had a wall built around your inner world. People had a hard time figuring you out. Why? You didn't talk enough! Communication stayed on safe subjects but didn't reveal much about the real you. Your privacy was too highly protected. You had such a strong defensiveness that others could not get close to you. You were often perceived as being secretive. You trusted few, and in some ways you didn't trust yourself enough to admit what you really needed in order to be happy. You were depressed in lives where you truly wanted a soul mate but were too fearful to come out of hiding. Denial about your need for love kept you alone.

Illumination for the Current Life

If any of these past-life patterns of the Capricorn First Zone are again with you in this lifetime, you can deal positively with them. You will need to be persistent and make regular effort to reverse their influences. Your commitment to overcome these behaviors will pay huge dividends!

In counteracting Climbing the Ladder of Success, you can still be ambitious. Being born in this First Zone of Capricorn puts you in the driver's seat, wanting to show off your ability. You attract responsibility without even really trying. Yet, you need to make time for other areas like hobbies and vacations. All work and no play is not in your best interest. It's important that you do not lose sight of the important people who really know you. You need to learn to focus on the individuals who support your pragmatic ambition. You will have a much better chance for romantic happiness if you learn to make time for your main allies. You need to schedule in the people who are important to you! Balance is a key ingredient to keeping your goals in perspective. When the chips are down or your luck is not so good, you may be glad you have your closest supporters nearby. It will be more fun to have a soul mate to share in your success and cheer you on to victory. If you return the favor and do the same for those key people in your life, they will be there for you when you need them.

The I Am the Boss feeling can be overcome by relinquishing some control over others. Lighten up! You benefit when someone is free to express their own views. Equality in your partnerships allows for clearer communication. Getting accurate feedback about yourself is better than people saying only what they know you prefer to hear. Trust comes with practice. If you are fearful of being honest, you need to get beyond that. You may be surprised at how good it feels to have someone who truly knows you. Your relationships deepen and the commitments are solidified through genuine dialogues. You don't have to trust everyone, but your most intimate partners need to know what's really going on inside of you. It is exhausting to always be in control. Learn to delegate responsibility to others. It takes a load off of you to not be so focused on being in control. You get energized with a new attitude. Empowerment comes through having the faith you can surrender a compulsive need to be the boss.

In The Tree That Would Not Bend pattern, you will be happier if you can learn to flow more with change. Nothing truly remains the same forever. It's a fact of life that change is inevitable. Your health might even get a lift by not resisting new life directions. People can't always adjust to your way of doing things. Compromise is one big key to solving this pattern. Also, listening to advice from others could be in your best interest, so don't stubbornly close your ears to new information. You will experience less tension in your relationships if you become flexible. Traditions and the past can still be valued, but don't make them your religion or only belief system. Perhaps building a new ritual or two will help reinvent your creative power!

The On My Guard propensity can be circumvented by opening up to the reality that you may not be happy shutting everyone out of your inner world. Privacy is a good thing, as it can recharge your mental, emotional, and physical batteries. However, privacy carried to an extreme dulls your mind and spirit. You need more stimulation, especially if you are feeling lonely. Let down the defenses and try an outgoing expedition. It's hard for people to understand you if you don't communicate. There is empowerment in talking! Expressing your views and—even more important—your innermost feelings puts you in touch with your intuitive power. It actually comes alive through verbalizing your thoughts. So try a change in strategy. You don't have much to lose except a few fears and bottled-up confusion. You can attract a more abundant and emotionally satisfying life by crossing over your guarded borders!

RoadMap to Your Empowerment

The First Zone of Capricorn is a great land for blazing a new ambitious trail. Being born in this sign zone blesses you with focusing power that many other sign zones envy. *The key to your personal empowerment is combining your pragmatic instincts with flexibility so you can adjust quickly to the changes required to ensure your success.* You naturally possess follow-through. Transcending your fears frees you to express your creative power spontaneously.

You enjoy your relationships more when you let others be free to discover their own true potential. It's just as vital that you be assertive in making your own needs known. A happy medium of give and take ensures fulfilling partnerships. You like individuals who are able to make their own way in the world. When you show a soul mate that you truly need their support, it deepens their sense of commitment. Carefully define your dependency needs, as this keeps the connection with others clearer.

Your road to happiness and fulfillment does not miss a beat when you learn to let your guard down. Try new experiences, even if they challenge your traditions and comfort zones. You grow stronger when you're not fearful of the future. Your goals stay fresh when your mind has faith in your ability. Don't feel you need to be in complete control. Life isn't meant to be lived that way. Success is more fun when you have people to share it with. Trust those you love and you never have to look far for a friend. The heights you want to reach are firmly in your grasp when you don't chase after them too hastily. Patience is your best teacher, yet acting on your instincts and not fearing a well-calculated risk might be the catalyst to offer you a renewed sense of self.

Second Zone of Capricorn: **12/31–1/9**
Element: **Earth**
Second Zone Sign Ruler: **Taurus**
Second Zone Energy Field: **Fixed**
Second Zone Signs: **Capricorn plus Taurus = Practical Values**

Current Life Scan for the Capricorn Second Zone

Your soul looked forward to a stabilizing lifetime filled with experiences that enriched your sense of self-worth. Being born in the Second Zone of Capricorn shows that you prefer to be in the company of people with logical minds. You like to know your closest friends and lovers can be counted on for dependability. You are a resourceful type with a keen eye for business. You have perhaps even more follow-through than the other two sign zones of Capricorn because your patience is a strong ally.

A primary drive is finding a creative expression that captures your vision of beauty and helps you find inner peace. You are driven to market your skills. Commitments are valued if you feel you can trust them. You like to put your time, money, and energy into what appears to offer a sound investment. Life seems more user-friendly when you don't grow too stubborn in your thinking. Flexibility is the lubricant that allows you to flow with change. Reinventing yourself during major life transitions gives you renewed energy.

You aren't one to give up easily in pursuing your dreams. It's your ideals that keep you young in spirit. Falling in love with a special person and with your favorite profession are keys to your fulfillment. You find greater self-discovery through not fearing new experiences. Not staying too attached to the past liberates your mind to think inventively and invigorates you to think with greater imagination about the present and future. Sharing your wealth of ideas and possessions with others expands your world into a stimulating landscape.

Past-Life Patterns for the Capricorn Second Zone

The past-life issues for you were connected to three themes. One was being *too controlling*; you feared not running the show. A second was *negative thinking*, which made you feel very low on inspiration. A third was a *fear of risk-taking*, which caused you to stay in limiting circumstances. You didn't always exhibit these behaviors, but your life was more difficult when you did.

Conditional Love

This wasn't you at your warmest. The underlying current was a firm desire to be in control. It caused you to conceal your affection for others. By being cold and distant, you hoped to manipulate others. You were too demanding of receiving love but not so good at returning it. Everything had to be earned from you in rigid ways. The rules kept changing to fit your own needs, which kept your partners and friends confused as to what you really expected. You were a lonely person. Even when living with someone, you lived in a solitary world. You were hard to approach. Breaking through to your emotional side was exhausting. You missed out on fulfilling relationships and friendships by not inviting people into your inner world.

I Give Up

When your thinking became overly negative, your life wasn't fun or creative. Behind the scenes in this pattern was low self-esteem. It made the roles you were playing disorienting and unfocused. Your mind grew dull and resisted new stimulation. Backing yourself into a corner of gloom made new life directions difficult to perceive. You didn't flow well with change, which was another side of the coin. New circumstances sometimes found you not willing to make the effort to start over. Often there were people in your life trying to throw you a life preserver of hope, but your unwillingness to receive help only served to prolong the problem.

No Momentum

When clouds of inertia settled in, there was not much moving forward in your life. Why did this occur? Occasionally it was a lack of ideals to fire up your enthusiasm. You were too attached to materialism and had little interest in the symbolism or dreams that could have lifted you to new heights. There were lifetimes in which you were so heartbroken by failed romances that you stopped moving. You were too idealistic and not reality-oriented enough to bounce back from failed relationships. There were past lives that found you just not having the faith to act on your instincts and ideas. You talked yourself out of going in new directions.

Playing It Too Safe

You got a little too complacent in some past lives. The familiar is all you wanted to stay confined within. You preferred no outside interference and business as usual. This did keep you in narrow realities that caused you to miss more options that were readily available. You were ruled by a fear of the unknown. You fought against innovative ideas that might have made your life exciting. Your relationships grew stale from sticking to the same old routines even if they bored you to death. You showed a stubborn defensiveness against change. Your loyalty to traditions was admirable but not always wise if it made new growth impossible to embrace.

Illumination for the Current Life

If these past-life patterns have resurfaced in the current incarnation, there are ways to overcome their influences. It will take regular effort to turn these behaviors into positive expressions. If you stay determined, it can definitely be done!

In the Conditional Love quandary, you need to consider a new approach in making others feel valued in the same way you want to feel valued. It will work wonders in creating harmony in your relationships. You can't approach love in the same exact way you approach business—the rules of the games are not the same. Business dealings are supposed to be impersonal or at least have certain understood ground rules; love needs certain definition as well, but feelings need to be expressed to let someone know how to get close to you. People will learn they can trust you if you show you really want an intimate relationship on the emotional level. Manipulating the rules to fit your own needs doesn't establish the kind of closeness you need. It may be a little scary at first to be honest about what you really need. Opening up your inner world to a special someone allows for the possibility of a long-term commitment that could prove to be quite fulfilling. If you are tired of being lonely, then adopt a new strategy in communicating your feelings. You have nothing to lose except your fears and isolation. There is much to be gained!

The I Give Up tendency requires that you stop sabotaging your positive energy with negative thinking. You may need to read books on the power of positive thinking. It takes a lot of energy to stay on the negative side of life. Actually, it is quite draining! So why not move over to a positive neighborhood in your brain? You will find yourself quickly energized with a new outlook. If someone is trying to help you out of your negativity, be sure to grab their hand and let them assist you. Don't fight change. It can stimulate your brain to move in new directions. If your feelings of self-worth are not as high as needed, you can get a quick increase by focusing on your own needs. Perhaps you are working too hard to make others happy and forgetting about yourself in the process. Believing in your inner strength to move past negative roadblocks can take regular practice. Let your intuition guide you. There is much inner power to tap into. You may need to get better at rewarding yourself. Learning that you are worthy of receiving the good things in life is a step in propelling you out of a negative mind-set.

The No Momentum pattern can be overcome by keeping your mind regularly immersed in new learning. You may need a challenge occasionally to get your fire ignited. Reality-testing your romantic idealism is not a bad idea. You don't want to believe so much in someone else that you can't move on when you are disappointed in them. Whatever type of loss you endure, you eventually need to find your footing once again. The physical world cannot always provide us with everything for happiness, but you have a vast inner world just waiting to inspire you. Developing your creative power can blast you forward in a hurry. Balancing your pragmatic perceptions of life with tuning into your rich inner world keeps you on target for greater fulfillment.

Conquering the Playing It Too Safe pattern doesn't require you to be James Bond or Superwoman, but it does mean you need to venture out beyond your comfort zone occasionally. You don't want to miss out on those new doors to self-discovery by always taking the same old roads. Your mind gets ignited into greater creative patterns when you allow for exploration of a unique path. Even your relationships are stimulated by exposing yourself to different scenery. Traveling to places you have never been or studying a subject foreign to your normal life can lift your spirits. Allow for new challenges—it keeps you mentally alert and your entire being gets revitalized through letting alternative experiences be part of your life. You may even find a way of reinventing yourself in an unexpected way by taking a walk outside of your usual routines.

RoadMap to Your Empowerment

The Second Zone of Capricorn is a terrain with ample space for your creative passion. It offers a serenity that can help you tap into ways to relax even in the middle of a demanding schedule. *The key to your personal empowerment is not being afraid of new challenges even if you are initially not sure how to respond to them.* It's your patient and methodical commitment to being a success that others admire. You are at your best when acting responsibly and yet able to see the humor in your life. Balancing work and responsibilities with taking time for pleasure keeps you young at heart.

Your instincts for business are above average, being born in this sign zone. There is an innate sense of beauty and love for nature that sensitizes your awareness. Your self-esteem is valuable to maintain. Knowing when to reward your efforts is just as vital to your happiness as is the very air you breathe. Remembering that positive thoughts are more replenishing than worries keeps you centered. If you lose momentum, you may need to reach back for a bit of self-confidence to keep you going. Don't forget there are always options in any problem. This is a great sign zone from which to find the solutions to any puzzling questions.

Give yourself permission to travel to ideas and places that give you new insights. Keep your mind curious and your body well nourished and you are well on your way to an exciting life. Your relationships blossom when you reveal your feelings. Learning to trust deepens your commitment. Testing your ideals to see if they are solid is wise. Don't be afraid to dream—dreaming is the gateway to your intuitive and creative power!

Third Zone of Capricorn: **1/10–1/19**
Element: **Earth**
Third Zone Sign Ruler: **Virgo**
Third Zone Energy Field: **Mutable**
Third Zone Signs: **Capricorn plus Virgo = Efficiency in Motion**

Current Life Scan for the Capricorn Third Zone

Your soul was ready to enter this incarnation to put a plan into action quickly. Being born in the Third Zone of Capricorn adorns you with a mind that doesn't like to take No for an answer when you are determined to finish a job. With Virgo ruling your sign zone, you do need to watch out for trying to make things too perfect. Learning not to worry about what you can't accomplish makes your paths smoother.

A primary drive is to find creative outlets that allow your imagination and knowledge to stay stimulated. Without stimulation your mind doesn't feel nourished. You have more nervous energy than the other two sign zones of Capricorn, so you need plenty of exercise and work that keeps you challenged. Just be sure you don't overburden yourself with responsibilities that could be delegated.

You like well-organized people. Lovers and friends who don't surprise you with unexpected stressful news are appreciated. You like to be well-prepared to handle adversity rather than meet it with no warning. Your nervous system is delicate. Taking care of your mental and physical health through an organized schedule agrees with you. If you have to adapt to a more hectic pace, it's in your DNA to make the adjustment. Your mind, body, and spirit stay in balance when you keep your expectations for yourself and others reasonable. You prefer new romantic partners (and even friends) who give you enough time to feel comfortable with the relationship. You are capable of long-term commitments because you do like establishing and honoring traditions. Keeping your options open allows you to have a more exciting life.

Past-Life Patterns for the Capricorn Third Zone

The past-life issues for you were linked to four themes. One *was being too strict* and denying yourself pleasure too much of the time. Another trend was *overworking*; you went too far beyond the call of duty. A third area was *extreme mental lows*, dwelling too much on what might go wrong. The fourth was a *lackluster idealism*, where you had trouble dreaming of a better tomorrow. When you got stuck in any of these patterns, life was more difficult to enjoy.

Austerity Trip

You did get carried away with denying yourself the finer things in life in more than one past incarnation. The reasons for this varied. Sometimes you were too tight with your money. You would not spend it on having a good time even if you were wealthy. You took saving for a rainy day to the extreme. There were other incarnations that featured low self-esteem, and that was the reason you didn't reward yourself enough. Then there were incarnations that found you making too many sacrifices for others. You ignored your own needs. Getting into relationships with controlling partners kept you from indulging in pleasurable activities. A lack of faith in abundance was an underlying current running through this pattern. You thought if you spent what you had it would never get replaced, no matter how hard you worked. Your mind had a tendency to focus too much on what you might lack rather than on what you had to empower yourself or others.

Work Crazy

Worshiping work as if it were the ultimate experience caused you to ignore the important people in your life. Your reality was totally focused on getting ahead in the material world. Great ambition often made you a great success, but your family and love life suffered the consequences of your professional devotion. You lacked balance. Your emotions were poured into the world of business. There wasn't much left for your romances or for those needing your emotional support. In some incarnations you felt quite lonely because you worked yourself into a corner of solitude. You didn't make the time to develop relationships because your investment was all in terms of land, dollars, and cents.

Sad Sack

You had a tendency to let your worries weigh on you too heavily. There was compulsiveness about not being able to get a negative situation out of your mind. Rather than processing toward objectivity, you wound up feeling quite low. Another side of this pattern was blaming yourself too much if things went wrong for others. You had extreme guilt complexes. An inability to redirect your negative thoughts into positive directions kept you stuck. You were not very good at asking people to help you out of depressing moods. Resisting help contributed to this pattern. You needed ideals to inspire you, but you lacked the energy to get moving. Sometimes it was having too much idealism and not enough reality-testing that got in the way of your clarity. Your sadness was due to being disappointed in someone you trusted or because a cause didn't live up to your expectations.

Lack of Imagination

The earthy side of your consciousness had trouble climbing to a high enough altitude to let your intuition guide you into inspiring territory. You fought against innovative ideas being offered to you. Change seemed threatening. You chose to hold onto what you knew rather than experiment with new ideas. You missed out on opportunities for greater self-discovery by remaining in the safe and familiar. A fear of risk-taking occasionally interfered with a new venture that might have sparked creative passion. It wasn't that you were lacking a sharp mind, it's that you were reluctant to step out and try new paths.

Illumination for the Current Life

If these past-life patterns of the Capricorn Third Zone have reactivated in this life, there are ways to make peace with them. You will need to make a committed effort to get past their influences. With practice and patience, it is possible to overcome them.

Solving the Austerity Trip pattern requires you to be freer with your money and possessions. Having more faith that the universe will replace what you spend liberates you from this pattern. Being too controlling of your resources holds you back. Investing in your future or that of someone you love is an inspirational experience. If your fear is due to low self-worth, then you need to start valuing your own needs more. It is amazing how fast you can turn around this behavior if you refocus your energy in a positive direction! Giving all of your power away to others only serves to hold you back. Reclaiming your power intensifies your creative energy in a big way. Separating yourself from overly controlling individuals ignites you into a whole new way of perceiving the world. Having greater belief in the power of abundance is something you must incorporate into your thinking. Adding things that would make your life more enjoyable is a good thing. It shows you love yourself. Saving and budgeting is fine, but be sure you balance these tendencies with rewards that make life more stimulating and peaceful.

The Work Crazy pattern requires that you learn moderation. Balancing work with relaxing experiences is good for your mental and physical health. Worrying that you will miss out on a business deal or the chance to make extra money if you take the time for other life experiences is not wise. Trusting that you can be financially stable without working all of the time lessens your stress. Having a schedule that doesn't use up all of your energy adds much needed vitality. There is a greater chance to enjoy your romance and family life if you keep your ambition in perspective. Paying yourself with a richer emotional existence as well as with dollars points the way to fulfillment on a higher level. You deserve more than material wealth alone. If you want to ensure you will not be a lonely person, focus more time on avenues other than your professional life. Enriching your schedule with exercise, travel, study, romance, and time spent with family is empowering and recharges you to work even better!

The Sad Sack pattern is best dealt with by not letting your worries dominate your thoughts. You lose a lot of solid creative energy letting it leak out by obsessing about situations you cannot control. It's actually easier to focus on something you *can* get a handle on: your positive thinking. When you don't give in to guilt over feeling responsible for other people's problems, you go far in stopping this pattern. It takes faith in yourself to stop feeling guilty. Let others take responsibility for their own mistakes or challenges. You can be supportive but need to know your boundaries. Watch how far you go in idealizing others— there are no perfect individuals. Stay realistic in your expectations. It's good to have ideals that keep you inspired. Staying open to new ideas and not being afraid to receive help can lift you out of sluggish moods.

The Lack of Imagination rut can be magically transformed into creative pursuits by letting your intuition have a voice. You have much more to gain than lose when you take a leap into unexplored territory. Life will be more fun and stimulating if you let new learning have a place in your life. Getting past a fear of change could invigorate your mind with great new insights. Learn from the past, but don't be ruled by it. Traditions are fine, and starting a new one can prove to be exciting and refreshing. Joining a new group or studying a new subject keeps your mind sharp. Let a friend or family member talk you into trying an alternative path. Variety will make you feel more alive and ready to meet the future with a whole new attitude!

RoadMap to Your Empowerment

The Third Zone of Capricorn is a solid terrain from which to launch your plans for the future. Being born in this zone means you have a razor-sharp intellect that can cut through any obstacles in your path. *The key to your personal empowerment is embracing change with courage and not worrying about the past.* Keeping your mind open to new learning prepares you to deal with the world's ups and downs.

Your sign zone ruler, Virgo, helps shape your ideas into marketable realities. An innate drive to see a goal through to the end is one of your strong points. Knowing when to scrap a plan and move in a new direction comes with experience. Flexibility makes you a more likeable person, and showing a sense of humor balances out your tendency to be overly serious. Expressing your work skills gives you a feeling of self-mastery. Making time for hobbies and relaxation recharges your mind.

Allow for your dreams to be as important as your logic and you are never too far from happiness. Your love life improves when you become a good listener and aren't afraid to communicate your feelings. Keep your mind full of positive thoughts and there is little room for sadness. Greet life challenges with optimism and there is less chance for self-doubt. Humbly ask that your intuition support your quest for self-discovery and you are never really alone. Believe in your talents and your creative power is only a breath away!

Aquarius: The Inventor

1/20-2/18

Traditional Astrology Phrase: "I Know"
Archetypal Theme: Conceptualization of Direction

First Zone of Aquarius: **1/20–1/29**
Element: **Air**
First Zone Sign Ruler: **Aquarius**
First Zone Energy Field: **Fixed**
First Zone Signs: **Aquarius plus Aquarius =**
Determined Independent Spirit

Current Life Scan for the Aquarius First Zone

Your soul entered this incarnation with an electrifying intensity. You were born in the First Zone of Aquarius, which points to a mind that never stops thinking! Your ideas pump as steadily through your brain as blood from your heart. The future is often where you reside. It is wise not to ignore the present or act like you don't have a past. You are blessed with inventiveness that many other sign zones look upon with admiration. Your enthusiasm to live each day as though it was an original experience is what drives you.

Your lovers and friends like your refreshing insights. They appreciate you even more if you support their goals. It's vital that you feel like an equal in your partnerships. Freedom is highly valued, as is friendship. Reinventing yourself from time to time is likely—you have done this over several lifetimes, so why would this one be any different? Learning patience doesn't come easily; if you have already mastered this, consider yourself lucky.

A primary drive is discovering a deeper sense of yourself through creative accomplishments and relationship connections. You like following the beat of your own drum. An unconventional heartbeat is your regular pulse. People with an ability to surprise you intrigue your mind. You probably talk and move faster than many, but when you decide to focus through the Fixed energy of your sign zone, you are as movable as a mountain. Some accuse you of being stubborn, though you explain it as being persistent. You like life to be on your own terms but will make concessions if someone can logically prove to you why you should adjust your thinking. You respect free thinkers. When you show a little emotion to those you care about, they tend to stay by your side through thick and thin. It's your impeccable devotion to cutting-edge trends that separates you from the crowd. You can be committed to a tradition but it needs to earn your trust by proving that it won't try to stifle you. A rebellious streak is never far from your mental impulses. Letting your closest friends, relatives, and lovers know your inner motivations earns their trust. You are a maverick in the true sense of the word. It stimulates you to know your life directions will keep you growing and learning.

Past-Life Patterns for the Aquarius First Zone

The past-life issues for you centered around three themes. One was an *extreme willfulness*; you had to get your own way or else. A second area was being *obstinate*; your zone energy field being Fixed is pointing to this as a previous incarnation behavior. A final trend was *escapism*; you ran from responsibility rather than deal with problems. This isn't saying you were always acting out these behaviors, but your life wasn't as rewarding when you did display these tendencies.

Different Just to Be Different

There were times you rebelled to the max. There wasn't any real purpose to making your ideas difficult to understand, you just wanted to confuse others with your actions. Disrupting the flow in your relationships purposely created great instability. Closeness was next to impossible because you were terribly unpredictable. Your goals were hard to make a reality because you lacked the patience to see them through to completion. You were determined to be unique, which in itself was fine. It was when you wanted to be perceived as different and unusual without showing any regard for the needs of others that this pattern became a big problem.

I Shall Not Be Moved

This was you at your most stubborn. If you made a decision, it could be like trying to move Mount Everest to get you to consider another point of view. There was a self-centered quality to this pattern that alienated people. You were a creative force. There wasn't any problem being a success in the world. People saw you as a negotiator looking out only for your own best interest, and that is what caused power struggles. Compromise was not your first thought, or your second. Being seen as right was another side to this behavior. You were a competitive type who didn't give in easily. Inflexibility didn't make you popular with friends, family, or lovers. You set your sights on a target or goal and there was no talking you out of it!

Self-Imposed Exile

You chose isolation at times in order to hide your feelings. There was a preference to keep things on an intellectual level. People noticed you could treat them as close allies one day and as distant acquaintances the next. You left good relationships or professions too quickly without giving them a chance. Impatience and a fear of commitment were the underlying currents at work. It was easier to hide your emotional needs than to risk hurt feelings. You detested rejection and so chose not to give someone the chance to reject you. It was your sudden change of direction that made it tough to really get to know you. In some incarnations, you were a bit of a lone wolf, not wanting to belong to a group or network of people. It was a lack of trust that kept you in isolation.

Escape into the Next Century

Your mind was in love with the future in this pattern. The present and past were not of importance to you. It was hard for you to slow down your thought processes and focus on current commitments. An inner restlessness dominated you. Hopping from one goal to the next rather than finishing what you started proved frustrating for you and those who depended on you for support. You were inventive and a bit eccentric. When your ideas veered too far from the mainstream, it was a challenge for people to follow your logic. Stability was not your main priority. As a matter of fact, you went out of your way to cause friction if life became too peaceful. Nervous exhaustion sometimes resulted from an inability to accept calmness as normal. Establishing roots or a solid home was problematic in some incarnations due to a constant craving for new stimulating experiences.

Illumination for the Current Life

If these past-life patterns are making themselves felt in this life, you can overcome their influences. You will need to be courageous and determined to transcend their negative impact. With regular effort and a little patience, anything is possible!

You can turn the Different Just to Be Different pattern into a more positive expression by showing others that you really hear them. Being born in this particular sign zone puts a great emphasis on developing your individuality. That's fine—just be sure you share the stage with those you truly care about. Accepting that stability is a good thing keeps you from sabotaging good relationships. Redirecting your passion for change and innovation into your creative pursuits takes the stress off of your partnerships. Your friends and lovers will trust you more if you clue them in on your sudden change of direction. Your goals are more easily put into action and then accomplished if you stay focused and disciplined. Fighting for your beliefs yields greater results if you are tolerant of opposing viewpoints. Your sense of identity deepens when you learn to patiently adapt to change. Your insights are better received when you take the time to carefully explain them.

In the I Shall Not Be Moved rut, you make more friends and encounter fewer power struggles by showing adaptability. You can't always expect others to adjust to your expectations any more than others should always expect you to do the same for them. Being a firm negotiator is fine. Be sure to attempt to create win-win solutions—they bring people to the bargaining table a lot faster. You are a happier person when changing from an unfulfilling life direction and moving to more fertile territory. Your staying power tends to be stronger than many other sign zones when you make a plan. Flexibility saves much wear and tear on your mind and body. Being perceived as having a strong spirit with a sharing heart takes you far in life. Learning to flow with life's ups and downs is a wise strategy. Knowing when you have fought long enough for an idea is better than pushing it far beyond its usefulness.

The Self-Imposed Exile pattern requires you to not shut out the people you want to get to know on deep, intimate levels. Your life gains greater depth through developing meaningful relationships. Creative doors of opportunity can be discovered by letting key individuals truly get to know the real you. Your intellect is usually powerful but your feelings stay hidden. Taking the risk of trusting someone allows you to have fulfilling romances and friendships. Try to be more consistent with closeness and people will trust you. Both your Sun sign and zone ruler are Aquarius, a sign known for being unique, so doing your own thing and having strong individuality came standard in this life for you. When you include someone in major decisions, he or she will want to stay a strong supporter of your needs. Sharing your knowledge and feelings goes far in keeping this pattern dormant or nonexistent.

The tendency to Escape into the Next Century can be neutralized if you find ways to focus on the here and now. You will find the future more rewarding if you honor your current and past commitments. You have a trend-setting mind. Your creative power intensifies in a good way if you discipline your mind to concentrate. Running away toward future goals only causes you to have to learn the same old lessons over and over again. It's better to deal with the problems and issues in front of you now. You can still dream and imagine a better life! Inner peace is worth valuing, as is some degree of stability. Your mental and physical health benefit greatly when you slow down. You will always need to keep your mind stimulated by exposing it to new challenges. Be sure to communicate clearly so the people you want to believe in you can understand your language.

RoadMap to Your Empowerment

The First Zone of Aquarius is exhilarating turf for the mind to explore life from many different angles. Being born in this zone indicates you enjoy future-oriented people. You aren't necessarily in a hurry to believe in someone else's causes. You prefer logical ideas that fit into your reality. *The key to your personal empowerment is having belief in your goals and enough patience to let your intuition guide you in clear directions.*

You believe in freedom and thrive on equality in your relationships. You find people with innovative minds stimulating. Incorporating flexibility into your thinking opens up new options. You are at your best when you don't feel limited by the choices you make. Then again, following through on commitments is wise. Your closest friends, family, and lovers will want to be supportive when they know you can be counted on during the best and worst of times.

Live in the present as well as the future. Taking care of current business prepares you for whatever comes your way. You were meant to turn your internal clock forward into the future. Cutting-edge trends might even excite you, and being an inventor is not out of your reach. Falling in love with the creative process is your key to success. Taking a thoroughly thought-out risk might just be the door to an abundant life.

Second Zone of Aquarius: **1/30–2/8**
Element: **Air**
Second Zone Sign Ruler: **Gemini**
Second Zone Energy Field: **Mutable**
Second Zone Signs: **Aquarius plus Gemini =**
Lighting-Fast Mental Impulses

Current Life Scan for the Aquarius Second Zone

Your soul was anxious to get the incarnation started! Moving in multiple directions at maximum speed was in the plan from the beginning. Your brain was implanted with the curiosity chip at birth, being born in the Second Zone of Aquarius. Ideas spring forward from your mind as gracefully as a seagull skimming the surface of the ocean, snatching a fish and flying briskly away. Your nervous system is delicate and doesn't like to be bombarded by too many worries at once. With Gemini as your sign zone ruler, you are capable of traveling in multiple directions simultaneously, more so than many other sign zones.

Your mind stays hungry for information. If you become bored for too long a time, you tend to lose interest in a project or job. People likely perceive you as a lively talker ready at a moment's notice to exchange ideas about a wide variety of subjects. Not getting scattered by having too much on your plate is a challenge. You attract individuals who want to use you as a sounding board. Be sure to get enough downtime to recoup your energy after long intervals of using your mind to solve problems and being on a job.

The key to your personal empowerment is learning to focus the intense surge of mental energy constantly available to you. Keeping positive thoughts filtering through you ensures that negativity will not become a close friend. Balancing your intellect and emotions is a lifelong quest. Self-mastery comes through acknowledging your faults and having the courage to face obstacles. You enjoy individuals with above-average communication ability. Fulfillment, love, and abundance are entirely possible when you maintain an upbeat outlook. Your lovers and friends will never wander away if you treat them as equals. You are at your best when living a life that offers you mental freedom and a stable living situation. Keeping your inner restlessness channeled productively points you toward a horizon that is user-friendly and full of rewards.

Past-Life Patterns for the Aquarius Second Zone

The past-life issues for you were connected to three themes. One was a mind that was in *extreme overdrive*; your thought processes moved too quickly. Another trend was *relying solely on your intellect*, when your emotions were missing in action. A third area was *extreme worry*; you could not stop thinking about your problems. When any one of these patterns became too prevalent, you were not very happy.

I Can't Slow Down

Your mind was racing so fast that you felt out of control in some past lives. The intellectual side of you was sharp, but the intuitive right half of your brain was not put into action enough. You needed this right brain pause to give you the advantage of resting your mental intensity. You became exhausted from not pacing your actions. Frustration resulted from this pattern because you felt like you were anxiously going in circles without getting much accomplished. Finding that inner center within your consciousness was a real challenge. Selecting unreliable friends and lovers only added to the confusion. You made bad relationship choices out of desperation, hoping a grounded partner might slow you down. This would have been a good plan if you had been in a calm enough state of mind to make this strategy work. You were not good at seeing your way out of the problems you created when you wanted easy answers to complicated situations.

I Think, Therefore I Am

You were a very intellectually oriented person as a rule in several past incarnations. A solid belief that you could talk your way out of anything was displayed regularly. Expressing feelings did not come naturally. Hiding behind your intellect did offend those wanting to know more about how you felt. You were a bit of a mystery in that you were so breezy with communication that you slipped away from emotional encounters easily. There were periods of loneliness when you refused to let anyone into your inner world. Your words did possess a biting sarcasm that caused tension with others. This was your way of showing anger. You didn't like direct confrontations and so tried to manipulate people through outsmarting them. Clear communication was avoided in personal relating when someone was trying to pry into your well-concealed feelings. When you showed little warmth, it cooled the hearts of those trying to understand you.

Nineteen Nervous Breakdowns

You had a mind that could climb Mount Everest, but you had an Achilles' Heel, or call it a breaking point. It's when you felt so overwhelmed by the stimuli, usually in the form of problems needing to be solved, that you fell apart. It would have been okay if you took the time for rest and relaxation. But guess what? You didn't! The result was a tired mind, body, and soul. You weren't as mentally sharp when running on empty. Your insights started to lose that beautiful luster you were known for. It became more difficult to take advantage of new chances for success when they presented themselves. Even your relationships broke down because you lacked the energy to truly be in them. Life wasn't as rewarding. You had a tendency to get depressed when your mind and body were depleted.

Stripping Your Gears

Shifting between gears too quickly and too often is not good for a transmission. This pattern could just as well been called *Procrastination Blues* or *Losing My Way*. When you moved on too many fronts at once, you got lost. The pressure got to you. Biting off more than you could chew got you into trouble. You tended to stop and get frustrated to the point of not moving toward a goal at all. Your mind was not able to shift into the right gear to get you moving again. The undercurrent was expecting too much from people and situations. You wanted fast results, but impatience didn't help matters; as a matter of fact, it made things worse. You actually had good long-range perspectives but tripped over those nagging details.

Illumination for the Current Life

If these patterns of the Aquarius Second Zone have recurred in this lifetime, there are ways to make peace with them. It will take some regular effort to get positive results and you will need to use a little of that Aquarius ingenuity to be successful!

In the I Can't Slow Down pattern, you need to learn how to get centered and stay cool in the midst of daily activities. The demands of life have a way of naturally speeding up your mental processes. You may find that meditation or other techniques to stay centered will help. Even exercise might be a way to get a handle on your energies—do whatever it takes to alert you that your mind is speeding out of control. If you are in the habit of being in relationships with people who push your panic buttons, then you need to look elsewhere for companionship. It all starts with you. It's true that having dependable partners is a great asset, and a solid, earthy friend or lover can help remind you not to panic. Try not to push yourself to move in too many directions at once. Learning to compartmentalize or take on only one thing at a time is a good idea. It would help you hit the brakes as needed. Give yourself permission to take a time-out when your mind feels like it is racing in the Indy 500. Collect yourself and recharge with a short break in the action. It would help you regain your composure and perspective.

The I Think, Therefore I Am problem requires that you express more emotion. Life gets very dry when you keep everything on an intellectual level. You would be wise to sprinkle in a little feeling now and then when talking to those you care about. It is easier for someone to feel the intimacy you want to achieve when you reveal more of your inner world. Don't ask that a lover or family member be a mind reader. Speak from the heart and you will get more heartfelt responses. Even your creativity deepens when you let some of that emotion speak through you. Let the passion of your feelings become visible. People will see that you truly mean what you say and thus will find you more charismatic. Your professional work would even benefit by showing more feelings. The creative power in you intensifies (in a good way) when you let that emotional center deep within have a greater voice!

You have to be bold in this lifetime and reclaim the power lost in the Nineteen Nervous Breakdowns pattern. It might be strange to think of giving up your power when you lose your way due to being a bundle of nerves. Getting hooked up to a reliable power source that replenishes your vitality is a must. How to do this? You must get good at listening to your body. Your intuition probably tries to send you warnings to relax, but an overactive mind bogged down with worry can drown out this inner voice. You owe it to yourself not to get exhausted. Don't push yourself past the breaking point. Set limits. Learn to decipher what in your life can be changed and what must be accepted as unchangeable, even despite your best efforts. Great worry won't alter the outcome of situations—it might even cause the final result to be more negative! Taking a positive approach is a good place to start. Try releasing your worries. Be warned: it takes a lot of practice to get good at this! Learn to have faith that things can work out for the best. Believing that a higher power can work things out for you is not so bad either. Make your best effort and then let go!

If you are continually Stripping Your Gears, you need to be more reasonable in what you expect from yourself and others. Taking the pressure off of you is a good start. You can get disappointed with the progress you make toward a goal if you overanalyze the process. The journey starts with the first step. Seeing the whole picture might be a talent you already possess. However, the devil can be in the details! Patience helps. If you tend to sit on a plan because the largeness of it scares you, breaking it down into smaller steps could be a benefit. You have a natural instinct to want to take off in several directions at once. Your sign zone ruler, curious Gemini, points to this. Focus comes more easily if you train yourself to target one thing at a time. Finishing one project can instill in you the confidence for another.

RoadMap to Your Empowerment

The Second Zone of Aquarius is a brisk terrain from which to create exciting new ideas for the future. It is a springboard from which to launch the plans that keep you very stimulated. *The key to your personal empowerment is to stay poised and centered when encountering new challenges.* That may sound like a contradiction: don't rush through projects, but it is okay to move quickly. This means to put your best foot forward without agonizing over every detail. Your mind tends to think lightning-fast. Pace yourself so you don't run out of energy before finishing what you begin.

Be open with your feelings with those you are close to. People need to know how you feel as much as they need to hear your verbal explanations. The exchange of ideas keeps you feeling young and fresh. Communication is a talent that can become a big part of your professional life and needs to be an active player in your more intimate relationships. You may find that travel and new learning will open you up to a larger world view. Exposing your intellect to many points of view makes you that much more able to handle new situations. Be a good listener so you can sense the pulse of the world around you. Your insights expand and flourish when you aren't afraid to taste the many experiences life has to offer. You are at your best when adopting an eclectic search for knowledge. It's then that life offers you its magic and can surprise you with love and abundance.

Third Zone of Aquarius: **2/9–2/18**
Element: **Air**
Third Zone Sign Ruler: **Libra**
Second Zone Energy Field: **Cardinal**
Third Zone Signs: **Aquarius plus Libra =**
Instantaneous Social Instincts

Current Life Scan for the Aquarius Third Zone

Your soul knew this was going to be an incarnation that featured meeting many interesting people. Being born in the Third Zone of Aquarius thrust you into an exciting world of social interaction. Maintaining your individuality while sharing your days with a romantic partner is a challenge. Keeping a delicate balance between fulfilling your own dreams while helping someone meet their own is maybe not easy, but it is an inward drive. Friends and family tend to lean on you heavily for guidance and perhaps you expect the same in return.

There is an appreciation for beauty in all of its forms that can lead to artistic expression. You prefer to put your own spin on what you create. Your professional skills mean a lot to you. When you show decisiveness, the world responds to your passionate self-expression. If you remain indecisive for too long, your self-confidence begins to wane. There are times you need a gentle push from within yourself (or from others) to take a risk that can open a new door of opportunity.

A primary drive is establishing an emotional sense of peace while at the same time forming rewarding partnerships. You naturally cut people enough slack to be themselves. Your first impulse is to trust a person unless he or she proves unworthy of your belief in them. Your initial impression of someone is often accurate, and denying what you see only gets you into trouble. A reality check on your dependency needs puts you on a road to clarity. Your heart is big and your mind is even larger. Letting your intellect be your sole guide as to what is best to investigate in life is not always the best policy; following your intuition and feelings might help you tune into transforming experiences. This life is full of surprises if you can keep your mind open to alternate possibilities.

Past-Life Patterns for the Aquarius Third Zone

The past-life issues for you were connected to three themes. One was a *self-serving drive for independence*; you weren't considerate of the needs of others. A second was a *loss of freedom* when you tried too hard to please others. A third trend was a *lost sense of direction*; emotional confusion got the best of you. This isn't saying you always portrayed these behaviors, only that your life was not as fulfilling when you did.

Don't Crowd Me

"Don't stand so close to me" might have been your mantra! There really wasn't anything wrong with making a strong statement about your love of freedom. You were a passionate lover and a revolutionary at heart. It's when you lost sight of those significant supporters and lovers while pursuing your own goals that you got off-track. You thought in terms of "having your own space" long before the idea was popular. You lost out on deeper commitments from loved ones because of the demands you placed on them. You weren't the easiest person to understand because you kept your insecurities and deepest needs a secret. The defenses guarding your emotions were very strong. Compromise was not one of your strong suits; negotiations had to be on your own terms all of the time. There was a stubborn streak that didn't exactly make you popular. It was difficult to help you because it wasn't easy for others to figure out what you needed. Your impulse to break away from close personal connections caused sudden disconnects in relationships.

Copy or Original?

In this pattern, you compulsively expected others to fulfill you, which of course was impossible. Your idealism was intense. It caused you to think someone else was so perfect that he or she would obviously make you deliriously happy. Your tendency to try to be like someone you idolized led you astray from your own identity. Wanting so badly to be loved or appreciated put you in relationships with people who were able to take advantage of your unconditional belief in them. You weren't really happy, in that your own needs went unfulfilled. Your creative power took a dip because you wasted so much energy being in partnerships that found you doing all of the giving and little of the receiving. Your independence was convoluted in relationships that swallowed up your freedom. You sometimes were too resistant to advice from friends and family trying to persuade you to leave these limiting circumstances.

Groupie

You loved causes. There were good ones and there were those that caused you to lose your sense of self-importance. Groups that empowered you were good, but there were affiliations that turned you into someone you were not. You became a representative of an organization without a clear sense of personal direction. The group mind or group thinking became your identity. This wasn't good for discovering your own life purpose. However, you were determined not to let anything shake you out of this thinking. Your options and opportunities were severely limited due to a narrow allegiance to a group that didn't have your own goals as part of their agenda.

Which Way Do I Go?

When you became too indecisive, you had a tendency to get extremely emotional about it. You lost the mental objectivity that was at your fingertips. Your mind was especially adept at seeing both sides of a choice. The problem was that you couldn't make up your mind. The longer you remained idle, the worse your confusion became. There was a tendency to back away from conflict. Rather than a direct approach, you chose to take the long way around an obstacle. This hindered your momentum to such an extent that you lost interest in what you were trying to do in the first place. Hitting the panic button occasionally made matters that much more difficult to straighten out. Your mind and emotions could be at opposite ends of the spectrum, pulling at one another in a tug of war–like battle. Getting grounded was a challenge when you became lost in a mental fog.

Illumination for the Current Life

If these Aquarius Third Zone patterns are still manifesting in this lifetime, there are ways to counteract their influences. It will take some of that good old-fashioned mental fortitude to get past them. With patience and practice you can accomplish this!

In the Don't Crowd Me pattern, you can still be that independent spirit you naturally enjoy being. Nobody can really take that from you. Having a wide circle of peers is stimulating. It's important that you stay conscious and very aware of the people in your life you depend on. Taking them for granted when things are going well is not wise. Your sign zone ruler, Libra, is a relationship-oriented influence that actually aids you in balancing your partnerships. Think in terms of equality and fairness and your friends will stay close allies. Having your freedom is a must. You need plenty of breathing space to maintain mental and emotional clarity. Just be sure to clue others in as to why you might need this latitude. Communication allows people to understand your needs. Making a few ground rules can be a good thing. Your lovers and friends may appreciate knowing what you expect of them. Expressing feelings lets someone see a deeper side of you. Letting your guard down now and then builds trust. If you want greater intimacy, be sure not to keep your inner world so closely guarded. You find inner strength through talking about how you feel.

The Copy or Original? problem is transcended through being true to your own identity needs. Seeing that there is no perfect person takes a lot of unnecessary pressure off of you. You can stop performing for others in hope of being accepted. Over-compromising is what got you into trouble in past lives. There must be equality. Your creative power finds greater energy when you aren't focusing all of your thoughts on making others like you. Believing people need to accept you as you are is a good positive affirmation. Some compromises have to be made in relationships, but you can't be the one making all of them and still find happiness. Your self-esteem will rise when your own goals get accomplished! There will be less of a tendency to trap yourself in partnerships where you do all of the giving. Experiencing an authentic you is refreshing and makes it next to impossible to want to fall back into this pattern.

If you like to belong to groups or causes, you only need to know your boundaries to stay clear of the Groupie pattern. Your own identity needs to stay polished and within clear view of both yourself and others. Causes can express your idealism. There is nothing wrong with this. Your values may inspire you to choose certain groups that symbolize them. Just be sure you don't let an organization take over your mind, body, and soul. There are limits to what a group identity can do for you. Maintaining a separate life outside of a group allows you to keep the two worlds from merging. You don't want a desire to be loved and appreciated to be your only reason to be part of a group. If you have a strong individuality and your own unique goals to guide you, then you are less likely to fall victim to surrendering your freedom.

Being decisive alleviates the influence of Which Way Do I Go? Training your mind to decisively pick from choices will make your life much less painful. It is agonizing to sit too long weighing options. Sooner or later you need to jump off the fence of indecision for the good of your mental and emotional well-being. Living with a decision, good or bad, is growth-promoting. You can always make a change later if the choice doesn't turn out to be in your best interest. Losing your sense of direction runs contrary to the Aquarian need to know where you are heading. You are lost without clear-cut goals. When you face conflict, your creative power is increased. You launch a new mentality that can reinvent you and make life more rewarding. Dealing directly with problems lessens the chance you will have to deal with the same scenario later. Taking the risk of believing in your choices steers you toward a life of fulfillment.

RoadMap to Your Empowerment

The Third Zone of Aquarius is an exciting land for creating new relationships and sharing what you value with a wide range of peers. You have a social grace that can attract abundance and the support from others you require. *The key to your personal empowerment is believing in your goals and being willing to share your knowledge with those you want as confidantes.* You have greater insights into the future when you balance your emotional and mental intensity.

Freedom and equality are likely highly valued. When you are clear about your identity, life flows. Trying too hard to please others causes you to lose your sense of direction. Being true to your own goals while at the same time offering encouragement to those you care about deepens your commitments.

Having confidence in your skills can propel you into new opportunities. Being decisive gives you a sense of ease when facing adversity. Meeting conflict rather than running from it deepens your sense of purpose. Listening to the opinions of others expands your mental horizons.

Going beyond a fear of communicating feelings frees you to be whatever you want to be. You are a liberated spirit when not waiting for permission to walk your talk. Finding a group or cause that symbolizes your belief system can be rewarding. Following the beat of your own creative drum excites you greatly. Sharing your life with a soul mate aligned with your appreciation for beauty, idealism, and peace is a joy that is hard to describe in mere words!

Pisces: The Dreamer

2/19-3/20

Traditional Astrology Phrase: "I Believe"
Archetypal Theme: Unifying Instincts

First Zone of Pisces: **2/19–2/28**
Element: **Water**
First Zone Sign Ruler: **Pisces**
First Zone Energy Field: **Mutable**
First Zone Signs: **Pisces plus Pisces = Intense Idealism**

Current Life Scan for the Pisces First Zone

Your soul knew this was going to be a lifetime of entering experiences that would excite your imagination. Being born in the First Zone of Pisces inspires you to be more idealistic and dreamier than most other sign zones. It doesn't mean you are not pragmatic when needed, only that you are fueled by deep emotions. *A primary drive is to believe in your highest values and have faith in your creative power.*

When you don't try to be too perfect, your life flows more easily. Your expectations of self and others must be kept reasonable. There is an inner urge to seek causes and creative outlets that symbolize your yearning for a feeling of wholeness. Your intuition can be quite strong and accurate. When your mind and emotions are balanced, your outlook tends to be positive.

Falling in love with a soul mate or a profession stimulates you to be upbeat. You are probably perceived by many as sensitive. You find greater stability when you accept that life has its ups and downs, its positive and negative periods, and is a great journey. Your mind is moved by creative individuals and someone not afraid to take a risk. Knowing your limits prevents you from acting without forethought. Self-confidence elevates your perceptions to a higher plateau from which to make your goals a reality. Learning to accept what you can't change and to tune into what you can change is true wisdom. Integrating your optimistic spirit with sound reality-testing keeps you focused. A feeling of inner peace and unity comes through knowing which life paths are mere illusions and which are the true reflection of your innermost needs.

Past-Life Patterns for the Pisces First Zone

The past-life issues for you were connected to three themes. One was a *fear of conflict*, where you didn't like dealing directly with problems. A second was a *lack of clear boundaries*; your dependency needs got out of alignment. A third trend was *extreme idealism* that blurred your mental perceptions. This is not saying you were always involved in these behaviors but only that when you did, life was not as fulfilling.

Don't Make Any Waves

You tiptoed around adversity as if it would disappear into the atmosphere if you ignored it. Denying there was anything wrong did not make problems go away. You frustrated your lovers, family, and friends by acting like everything was okay. Your refusal to listen to others about their concerns caused great tension in your relationships. Sometimes you were too afraid of hurting someone's feelings and that is why you portrayed this behavior. On other occasions, you were so sensitive that you didn't like discord to disrupt your emotional well-being. Hiding from trouble only caused issues to get bigger. You often had a strong creative streak but lacked the faith to meet life directly.

Emotional Savior

Your dependency needs were too tied to what you thought others needed. There was an intense desire to try to make everything okay for your favorite people. This in itself was not a bad thing. It's when you neglected what you needed in the process of rescuing people that you got off-track. Your mental clarity was drowned out by your emotions. You lacked balance and a grounded perspective. The result was lost time, resources, and energy. You became drowned by ignoring your limits. An underlying feeling of guilt was the driving force. There were individuals who were perfectly willing to take advantage of your generosity, and they weren't very good at giving back to you.

There was another side of this coin where you were the one doing all of the receiving. You were good at playing the sympathy card and feeling sorry for yourself. You expected others to do most of the giving and you did not give much in return.

Love Is Blind

You lacked a clear definition of boundaries. Your idealism was a dominating force. Reality-testing was absent, which caused you to enter relationships haphazardly. Stability was lacking because you were in partnerships that did not have a solid commitment to hold them together. When the intensity of the romance calmed down, the bond between you and someone else was not strong enough to sustain the relationship. There were lifetimes that found you not liking the work that a serious relationship took. You preferred running toward another adventure to satisfy your romantic yearning. You enjoyed the high that love could offer but not the demand of a real commitment. There was no desire to develop the clarity to find a long-term meaningful partner when this pattern was a strong player.

Rose-Colored Glasses

In this pattern, you looked at the world through lenses that wished to see only perfection. This made it difficult to be satisfied with what you had in your life. There was a divine discontent that permeated your thinking, which made it a real challenge to be content no matter how much you owned. People couldn't live up to the high pedestal you placed them upon. Your expectations were too unreasonable. You lived through long periods of sadness when you were not able to cope with the reality that life was dealing you. Your momentum to reach your goals slowed greatly when you gave up due to feeling that you could never perform perfectly.

Illumination for the Current Life

If you are dealing with any of the Pisces First Zone past-life patterns, there are ways to make peace with them. You will need to be determined to overcome their influences. Regular practice and patience is required.

To overcome the sway of Don't Make Any Waves, you need to face your problems in a more direct manner. Your creative energy and mental clarity will feel like they have had a tuneup if you don't back off from challenges. When you take the long way around obstacles, you waste precious time. It's true that rushing impulsively isn't the best policy, and not thinking before moving can prove unwise. But a regular practice of hiding how you really feel about situations works against you. People will be more supportive of your goals if you give them a better idea of what you need. If you are too sensitive, you may need to take a risk occasionally and look adversity straight in the eye. You will be surprised to find courage you didn't know you possessed. Showing that you really hear the problems someone is communicating to you builds trust. You may not even need to be the fixer—just listening can open up doors to greater intimacy and closeness.

In the Emotional Savior pattern, you need to take very good care of your boundaries in relationships. It's better not to enable others to lean on you too much. You pay too big a price for always being there to save someone from their problems. Balancing your mental and emotional energies is wise. Clarifying your dependency needs is a liberating experience that frees you to fulfill your own goals. Be sure you have friends and lovers who won't take advantage of your good actions. There needs to be some degree of equality in terms of giving and receiving. If you are always focusing on being the support system for someone, you neglect your own needs. On the other hand, if you do all of the receiving and give little back to others, it throws your partnerships out of balance. You need to be an independent spirit able to make your own decisions. Only then you can be a clear-headed friend or lover joining forces from a position of shared power. Your identity and life purpose are clear when you have well-defined dependency needs.

The Love is Blind tendency can be transcended by being willing to see! Taking a closer look into identifying whether your needs are truly being met in your relationships is essential to happiness. A realistic assessment of your partnerships may be painful, but at the same time can be very insightful. There is a wonderful feeling that occurs when you fall in love, an emotional high. It's the follow-through and dealing with the ups and downs of a relationship that deepen the commitment. You may find that you enjoy having someone in your life for a long shared journey. You discover more about your identity the deeper the connection with someone. Having some of your inner fears revealed by being in a close partnership can actually point you toward transforming self-discovery. Having the belief in yourself that you can sustain a long-term relationship is empowering. It's vital that you don't deny your needs to make a relationship continue. You are better off leaving a confining situation where you can't be yourself. Trusting your intuition may be part of the answer in learning how to decipher the right type of person for you. Self-honesty isn't easy in matters of the heart, but it can free you to move in a better life direction with a meaningful purpose.

The Rose-Colored Glasses pattern can be overcome through being willing to rethink perfection. You need to give yourself a break. There is no way anyone can live a life that perfectly matches what you need. You will never be able to find that perfect person, job, or even house. Everything takes some adjustment on your part, some degree of compromise. Making your expectations more reasonable sets you up for a life that can deliver inner peace and abundance. Redefining your goals might be necessary to meet the needs of the present. Don't live in the past and what you thought it should have been. You will be less disappointed if you can reassess how you can successfully turn what you have into a winning situation. The world will seem like a happier and friendlier place if you allow your idealism to make peace with reality. They can coexist as equal partners!

RoadMap to Your Empowerment

The First Zone of Pisces is a place from which dreams radiate. There aren't too many sign zones that can rival your intuitive power. Your imagination is vivid, as is your idealism. Sound reality-testing helps you balance the real from the unreal. *The key to your personal empowerment is self-honesty and having enough faith in your highest ideals to pursue your most heartfelt goals.*

Don't fear confrontation. It only strengthens your spirit to deal with issues as they arise. You are like a sponge when it comes to soaking up the energy of others, so knowing your boundaries is a must. Be clear when you have given much more than you've received. Giving back support to those you love is rewarding. Clarifying dependency needs points you toward paths that can only lead to the fulfillment of your goals.

You enjoy fun-loving, creative people. They keep you feeling inspired and young. Falling in love sparks your creative power, as does pursuing your most cherished values. Stay focused in developing your skills. You require work and life roles that enliven your emotions. A quest to live out your ideals comes as standard equipment in this sign zone. Keep your mind accenting the positive, and the love and happiness you seek is never far from your reality.

Second Zone of Pisces: **2/29–3/10**
Element: **Water**
Second Zone Sign Ruler: **Cancer**
Second Zone Energy Field: **Cardinal**
Second Zone Signs: **Pisces plus Cancer =**
A Longing for Home and Security

Current Life Scan for the Pisces Second Zone

Your soul knew this lifetime was a special opportunity to make use of a powerful intuition. Being born in the Second Zone of Pisces shows you have a sensitive emotional nature. Your moods are deep and can act as a barometer of how you are feeling. Your creative power rests heavily on how comfortable you feel with your life choices. *A primary drive is finding people and places that you feel can deliver fulfillment.*

You don't like to be pushed to move fast. Processing information first and then taking action is probably more your style. When you find interests that awaken your passion, you do tend to put your heart and soul into them. You find it easier to trust people with similar values. A desire to settle down with a special someone is important to you.

Privacy is godlike to your mind. You like individuals who respect your need for space so you can collect your energy. When you communicate your feelings, friends and lovers understand your needs better, although you sometimes wish a person could just tune into your thoughts rather than have to do a lot of explaining.

Your professional aspirations are high. You like displaying your thorough knowledge about a skill learned. Sharing your insights is stimulating. You attract success by having faith in your ability. Abundance follows your positive thinking. Happiness and a sense of security are never far off when you trust your intuition.

Past-Life Patterns for the Pisces Second Zone

The past-life issues for you were linked to four themes. One was *confused dependency needs*. You sometimes displayed extreme neediness causing emotional confusion; another side of this pattern had to do with giving too much attention to others. A second area was *running away from responsibility*, where you preferred taking the easy way out. A third trend was *lacking assertion* and fearing your own power. A fourth theme had to do with having *hidden agendas*. This isn't saying you always portrayed these behaviors, but that life wasn't as rewarding when you did.

Helpless Victim

You wanted to be taken care of a little too much. You had a way of manipulating others into feeling sorry for you. Your dependency needs became skewed by wanting to be on the receiving end of love, but you weren't good at returning that love. This caused your relationships to get out of balance. You lost more than you gained in this behavior, as it lessened your creative power. A loss of momentum in pursuing your goals was often the result. You tried to live out your creativity through the work of others. Your identity was not as clear because you looked to have others to fulfill you.

There was a flip side to this pattern. In some incarnations, you were placed too much in the caretaker role. You were the one taking care of people who were pretending to be helpless or extremely needy. Your boundaries were blurred, often out of guilt or feeling too responsible for others. You enabled them to be weaker and show less independence than they could have. Your strength was heavily relied upon and at times you were totally drained from letting others use your energy.

Cold Feet

This was more a lack of assertiveness than anything else. You feared moving into new growth when it required adjusting to change. You were tenacious about holding onto the past. The old traditions were what inspired you, and this in itself was not a bad quality to possess. It's when there was a culture clash between innovation and your old-fashioned thinking that you missed out on opportunities, since you clung to ideas born in the past. You wanted to run as far as possible from people trying to get you to open up to a path of alternative self-discovery. When your intuition tried to coax you into considering bold new paths, your mind insisted on listening to the voices of what you already knew, whether those voices brought fulfillment or not.

This pattern surfaced in some lives when you had trouble with trust. Your relationships were not as successful in this instance. Letting someone know your deepest feelings scared you. When a lover wanted to know more about your inner world, you withdrew from the relationship. You were difficult to get to know on an intimate level when hiding your emotions. The warmth you could have had was lost in a cold solitude.

The Great Escape

This surfaced as a fear of responsibility. You detested commitments in this pattern. If life got too demanding, you wanted to run to a new adventure. Being confined to the expectations of someone else got on your nerves. This made it a real challenge to develop a long-term relationship or build a profession. It was hard for you to agree to a long-range plan. There was a deeper underlying problem at work here: you were an absolute perfectionist! Nothing was ever quite good enough. You were a harsh judge of your own performance and weren't very fair to others. Having a sharp critiquing eye that lacked objectivity worked against you. It caused you to leave good situations too early because you found fault. You chose to sabotage your opportunities as an excuse to break free.

Sounds of Silence

Woven into the fabric of this pattern were hidden agendas. You didn't like to announce or give advance warning about your plans to others. Your main motivation was to perceive what benefited you. There wasn't enough concern about what might help someone else. This of course did cause anger and resentment when it became a constant behavior. Giving others the silent treatment when you were angry didn't do much to resolve your differences. Your moods became so intense that they fogged your reasoning power. You depended too much on others figuring out what was going on in your mind. Your need for space and privacy was used as a defense mechanism in order to cause confusion rather than clarity. When you did take time alone, it was too often spent sulking and feeling resentful rather than reflecting and getting recharged.

Illumination for the Current Life

If these Pisces Second Zone patterns are active in this lifetime, you can overcome their influences. It will take some practice and patience, but you can do it! If any of these behaviors have been recurring over several incarnations, it could take even more time to resolve them.

In the Helpless Victim pattern, you will find that well-defined boundaries are going to save you much time and energy. Your relationships are healthier when the expectations are clear. You and a partner each have your needs met when equality fills the air. Your goals have more power behind them when you aren't spending so much time plotting how to use the resources of others. Mutual empowerment creates win-win situations in your friendships and romances. If someone else is playing the victim, you don't want to always be taking on too much responsibility for others when they could be doing some of the work themselves. It's better to let others make their own mistakes so they can learn from these experiences. You can only protect a person so much. It's better to offer your support and be a cheerleader without making all of their decisions for them. Don't let guilt be the motivating force causing you to fall into this pattern. You need to have the faith that you are doing what's best for someone by encouraging the person to walk their own talk.

Cold Feet can be thawed by believing in your ability to break through to new self-discovery. It's okay to be true to past beliefs. Think of it as integrating the old and the new so you can take advantage of new possibilities. If you lack assertiveness, it does take practice to become bold about stepping into new territory. Taking small steps into a future filled with better alternatives is better than holding on too tightly to what is no longer working for you.

If you are timid about making new friendships or romantic partnerships, you may need to challenge yourself to give it a try. Sometimes breaking the ice is a matter of warming up to a new experience. Trust doesn't happen overnight. It takes time to build this with someone. Have fun with the process of making new acquaintances. Feelings and emotions scare everyone a bit. You don't have to be the greatest at sharing your inner world with a person, but even opening up just a little attracts warmth and trust from others. Your creative empowerment is enhanced by letting your innermost feelings be known. It can be the doorway to happiness and greater wealth on many levels!

The Great Escape pattern requires you to learn to follow through on commitments. Why? It adds to your ability to focus. It doesn't mean you have to stay in the same relationship or job forever. A feeling of permanency or belonging is a grounding force you need to cultivate. It deepens your identity and points the way to fulfillment. If perfectionism is a thorn in your side, you need to lighten up in terms of what you expect out of life. It's impossible to have perfection constantly manifest in a person, place, or thing. This doesn't mean you can't put your all into doing an excellent job, it's just that you need to know when your best effort is good enough. Don't be as hard on people or on yourself as you are on your problems. Stay positive in thought and you will find others wanting to be supportive and working with you. If you grow too critical of their imperfections, you will cause tension and power struggles. Make your goal that of harmony and unity and you stand a better chance of achieving happiness. Be content with your most sincere effort and you are already a good way toward healing this pattern.

The Sounds of Silence pattern can be neutralized by being more direct in your communication. Talking is better than staying so quiet that you confuse yourself and others. Verbalizing is part of the path to processing information with your friends, coworkers, family, and lovers. Silence has a purpose as part of reflecting, but it still takes actual exchanges of words to get clear results. It isn't wise to make someone feel guilty by hiding your feelings. Take time alone to collect your thoughts if that is needed, but eventually come back to the negotiation table and talk it out. If you brood while retreating, you can think of it as a form of venting. But if you do this for too long, it causes you to lose time and energy. Holding your emotions inside causes them to either cloud your mental clarity or make you verbally explosive. It's better to have a balance between privacy and coming out into the open and talking. You are a passionate person and don't need to hold your anger inside. Let your feelings out! Your mental and physical health benefit from channeling this powerful energy productively.

RoadMap to Your Empowerment

The Second Zone of Pisces is a climate filled with deep emotions. Your creative power is fueled by your feelings and intuitive instincts. There is a love of past traditions and a sincere loyalty felt toward those supporting your most cherished beliefs. You experience greater self-discovery by embracing the present and future with an eagerness to learn. *The key to your personal empowerment is having faith in your talents and expressing your innermost feelings with those you love.*

You can't shoulder all of the responsibility in relationships, nor can you expect others to carry an unreasonable load for you. Balancing your dependency needs keeps you on the road to prosperity and happiness. You crave privacy because it makes you feel secure. Your soul mates must honor your need for distance and yet tolerate your sudden occasional need for closeness. You must do the same for them to maintain trust and a close bond.

The mysteries of life can be fun and exciting to explore. You thrive on a life filled with new challenges. Accepting that stability is okay is a wise move. Moving beyond your comfort zone takes courage but the rewards are great. When you don't run away from conflict, you find inner strength. Making your ideals visible accelerates your empowerment. Following that inner voice telling you to seek paths that make you feel alive and vibrant opens doors you'll never regret walking through!

Third Zone of Pisces: **3/11–3/20**
Element: **Water**
Third Zone Sign Ruler: **Scorpio**
Third Zone Energy Field: **Fixed**
Third Zone Signs: **Pisces plus Scorpio = Penetrating Intuition**

Current Life Scan for the Pisces Third Zone

Your soul looked forward to a life of deep inner self-discovery. Being born in the Third Zone of Pisces indicates you have intense emotions that need to be directed productively. The journey might not be easy but each challenge you greet courageously is full of rewards. *A primary drive is maintaining a positive life perspective when faced with adversity.* You attract greater support from the universe for your goals when not overidentifying with negativity. You don't miss a step when believing in your ideals and trusting your creative instincts.

This Pisces zone is more focused than the previous two. People probably perceive you as determined to make your idealism become a reality. You appreciate loyal friends, lovers, and family members. There is a strong tendency to bond deeply with those you love. Your faith in others can be a catalyst for their success. You only ask that they show the same belief in your goals.

Self-honesty is a key to keeping your mind and feelings clear. Talking truthfully and expressing your innermost yearnings to those individuals you value brings them closer to your heart. Dealing with past problems sets you free to enjoy the present. Conquering your fear of change is liberating. You came into this life to experience rebirths—often when you don't expect them! Perceiving life as a process containing mysterious forces waiting to be explored makes your days stimulating. When you don't dwell too long on an obstacle in your path, you find wisdom. It's in letting your intuition guide you to more peaceful and unifying waters that you reach great happiness. Balancing your dreams with reality makes for stability. Keeping your mind open to new ideas enlivens your imagination. Love and abundance are frequent companions when your eyes look to the future with a hunger for growth.

Past-Life Patterns for the Pisces Third Zone

The past-life issues for you were connected to four themes. One was *manipulation through silence*; by not letting your ideas be known, you hoped to control people. A second trend was *lost idealism*, when your dreams disappeared. A third was being stuck in *emotional confusion*; your mind was flooded with too many worries. A fourth area was *denial* that warped your sense of reality. This isn't saying you always took part in these behaviors, but only that you were not as happy when you engaged in them.

Mime

You were stone silent when you wanted to be. Why? There were occasions when you felt like forcing someone to your way of thinking by giving them the silent treatment. This was your way of voicing displeasure. Rather than openly showing anger, you found it more useful to get what you wanted by simply not responding. This was sometimes a technique utilized to distance yourself emotionally from others. Also, it was a self-serving behavior in that you were only thinking of your own needs. Rather than express feelings, you stayed quiet. Trust was not your strong suit when playing out this hand. Your relationships tended to lack depth due to poor communication. You had a great fear of being honest. You didn't want to risk getting hurt, and a fear of rejection was at the heart of this pattern. Loneliness was too often your dance partner.

Paradise Lost

When you succumbed to extreme negative thinking, you fell into this pattern. You had a strong dose of idealism in your mental chemistry. It wasn't the ideals that got you into trouble, it was not being able to accept reality when a cherished dream fell apart. You didn't cope well with disappointment. Or perhaps it's more accurate to say you didn't bounce back from circumstances that didn't go your way. You leaned toward compulsively directing your mind at the negative. Positive thoughts were nowhere on the horizon. A nagging voice in your head urged you toward perfection. You lost hope when a plan didn't develop exactly as you imagined it should. A goal may have been successful with some patience, but you impulsively rushed to the judgment that all was lost. Your resistance to positive outlooks kept abundance and wonderful opportunities at bay.

Treading Water

Your emotions were larger than life. You had a wonderful intuition. So where was the problem? Trouble came in when you stopped believing in your abilities. A lack of faith is what derailed your goals. You had intense ambition but kept it locked up in an inner chamber. Your lack of focus caused your mind to be soaked in confusion. Your life came to a sudden standstill. You were not easy to budge out of fixed attitudes. When people threw you a life preserver, you didn't reach for it. You wanted to be your own person and solve life's dilemmas on your own terms. People perceived you as stubborn, though you explained this as being determined. Frustration often became more your reality than fulfilling your dreams.

Coloring the Truth

Denial was at the root of this one. You liked to paint your reality according to what you pretended it should be, rather than what it was truthfully. This did cause you to enter relationships that often were not in your best interest. By refusing to see people as they actually were, you lived in a world of make-believe. You were not treated as an equal and your own needs were taken for granted. Low self-esteem was the motivating factor in this behavior. It kept you from being assertive for your own goals. Your hopes and wishes took the back seat.

Illumination for the Current Life

If these Pisces Third Zone patterns are a recurring problem in this lifetime, there are ways to get around them. It will take a regular commitment to make peace with them. If any one of the behaviors has been with you over several incarnations, it will take a little extra effort to get positive results.

In the Mime habit, you need to understand that there is a time for remaining quiet to contemplate, but there is also a need to eventually make your needs visible. Rather than expecting others to read your mind, you will get much better results through honest communication. Intimacy is achieved by sharing your feelings. To build trust with those you love, it is vital that you don't hide your emotions. Being a Water sign, your creative power gets ignited and stays inspired through emoting! Even your immune system gets a boost when you talk. People will like you more if they get the idea you are not trying to manipulate them through staying silent. That's why it's best to keep your plans and ideas out in plain view. In business dealings, the rules are different. You do have the very focused sign of Scorpio as your sign zone ruler, which indicates you can become passionate about pushing a professional agenda. You may have already perceived that you do need to hide a card or two in dealing with the pragmatic business world. On the playing field of love and friendship, though, remember to switch gears. You can give yourself permission to open up your inner world to people needing access to it. It deepens your bond with them. Balancing your need for privacy and disclosure is the way to silence this pattern!

The Paradise Lost pattern asks that you don't let an extreme drive for perfection impede your progress toward achieving your goals. You need to toughen up a bit as well. Life will not always open its doors to your most heartfelt dreams immediately. Rejection doesn't have to mean the end of a plan. Being determined and—even more important—believing in your ability are key ingredients to happiness. Patience is helpful. Understanding that life is a process of self-discovery as well as trial and error is wise. Positive thinking goes far in neutralizing the influence of this pattern. You are being drained when you obsess over what you do wrong or overthink problems. Pouring your mental energy into positive thoughts attracts the abundance and fulfillment you seek. So reclaim your power by resisting the temptation of negative thinking. It can be accomplished through constantly reminding yourself that you want to meditate more on the goals in front of you rather than the ones you left behind.

Kicking the Treading Water habit requires that you keep moving, even when frustrated. We all go through time periods when our best efforts aren't getting the desired results. That's no reason to stop believing in your ability. You are blessed with a powerhouse of intuition in Pisces and a rugged determined spirit in Scorpio. This is a winning combination that makes you able to handle adversity in whatever form it takes. Get better at receiving help if that's an issue. Nobody can truly go it alone in life. Let someone you trust give their support—it may be the fire that rekindles your momentum. You might need to learn how to meditate or at least learn a technique to tune into your inner world. Staying centered and yet mobile is the key. If you are a sensitive and idealistic type, it's important that you don't let the world dampen your spirit. Keeping the faith may take some effort. The payoff for taking even small steps toward your goals far outweighs worrying about what you can't do!

If you are Coloring the Truth, you could get better results by not denying the reality of situations. This only causes you to prolong problems and keep yourself locked into dead-end circumstances. It's wise to practice trying to perceive people as they really are, rather than what you want them to be. You have a vivid imagination that can be well-utilized creatively. Just be sure to channel it accurately when it comes to sizing up people. You need relationships that offer you equality and enhance your self-esteem. Building stable partnerships depends on your clear assessment of how you are actually being treated. It is essential that your own needs get the same support you are offering to others. The giving and receiving need to be balanced.

RoadMap to Your Empowerment

The Third Zone of Pisces is an oasis of creative pleasure. It does require a reality check now and then to keep your goals on target for their correct destination. Being born in this emotionally intense zone inspires you to courageously pursue your ideals. *The key to your personal empowerment is having faith in your insights and acting with decisiveness.*

Communicating your feelings with those you love deepens the trust. Remember to vocalize your ideas so others will understand the motivations for your actions. You have a strong desire to be treated as an equal. Finding mutually empowering partnerships, whether they be in business or in romance, is essential to your sense of fulfillment.

When you don't live in a state of denial, the world is a wondrous place in which to live out your dreams. Keeping your expectations reasonable allows you to find harmony in your professional life as well as in romantic aspirations. You have good business instincts that are lined with staying power. Your drive to finish a project or plan depends on how long you feel passionately committed. Life is more fun when you keep your desire for perfection within reason. You find a sense of renewal and rebirth through discovering your hidden talents. Don't ever fear trying a new endeavor because it might be just the ticket to newfound self-discovery!